TALES FROM THE
USC TROJANS
SIDELINE

TALES FROM THE
USC TROJANS
SIDELINE

A COLLECTION OF THE GREATEST TROJANS STORIES EVER TOLD

BY

TOM KELLY

WITH

TOM HOFFARTH

FOREWORD BY

CRAIG FERTIG

Copyright © 2007, 2012 by Tom Kelly and Tom Hoffarth

All Rights Reserved. No part of this book may be reproduced in any manner without the express written consent of the publisher, except in the case of brief excerpts in critical reviews or articles. All inquiries should be addressed to Sports Publishing, 307 West 36th Street, 11th Floor, New York, NY 10018.

Sports Publishing books may be purchased in bulk at special discounts for sales promotion, corporate gifts, fund-raising, or educational purposes. Special editions can also be created to specifications. For details, contact the Special Sales Department, Sports Publishing, 307 West 36th Street, 11th Floor, New York, NY 10018 or sportspubbooks@skyhorsepublishing.com.

Sports Publishing® is a registered trademark of Skyhorse Publishing, Inc.®, a Delaware corporation.

Visit our website at www.sportspubbooks.com

10 9 8 7 6 5 4 3 2 1

Library of Congress Cataloging-in-Publication Data is available on file.
ISBN: 978-1-61321-230-1

Printed in the United States of America

CONTENTS

Foreword vi
Introduction: THE MONTH WAS JUNE; THE YEAR WAS 1961. ix
Chapter 1: ASHLAND, IRONWOOD, DULUTH, DES MOINES, PEORIA 1
Chapter 2: SOUTHERN CALIFORNIA, 1961 11
Chapter 3: THE FOOTBALL COACHES 16
Chapter 4: OTHER USC NOTABLES 38
Chapter 5: THE NOTRE DAME MYSTIQUE IS NO MISTAKE 55
Chapter 6: A DOZEN GAMES, PLAYS, AND PLAYERS FOR THE AGES 64
Chapter 7: FOR YOUR CONSIDERATION 91
Chapter 8: UNFORGETTABLES: PLAYERS WHO DESERVE RECOGNITION ... 101
Chapter 9: THE NEAR MISSES 111
Chapter 10: PEOPLE, PLACES, AND THINGS 117
Chapter 11: LONGTIME FANS 156
Chapter 12: KELLY'S COLLEAGUES SPEAK UP 159
Chapter 13: AS USUAL, KELLY GETS THE LAST WORD 185
Acknowledgments 190
Index 195

FOREWORD

I FIRST MET TOM KELLY as a sophomore at USC in 1961, when Coach McKay introduced him to us during spring practice. He was Chick Hearn's new "phenom" color man from Peoria. They say if you can play in Peoria, you can play any stage—and that's been proven by Mr. Kelly.

Coming off a 6-4 year, our team wasn't too good at that point. But Tom captured us right then with his love for the game and his feel for us as a team. That's when the Voice of the Trojans was born.

He made a lot of people remember our names. Because of the way he'd describe the situation in a game, the magnitude of the next play kept the drama going.

And he was a man always prepared. I remember waiting for transportation the Friday night before a game in Illinois. Coach McKay was not a patient man, and our bus had broken down. Tom found a way to get a city bus to pick us up and take us downtown to see the movie *Rosemary's Baby*. On the way back to our hotel, Tom regaled our team with stories and songs—he was a real vaudeville guy. We all knew he was a celebrity in Peoria, and that night he showed it. The next day we went out and beat Illinois.

Somewhere in this book, you'll read about that USC win over Notre Dame in 1964. Without Tom, I never would have known what had happened. When I threw that pass downfield on that fourth-and-8 play with 1:50 to go against the undefeated and No. 1 Irish, I only heard

Tom Kelly and Craig Fertig celebrate their enshrinement into the USC Athletic Hall of Fame in 2001. *Photo courtesy of Tom Kelly*

what was happening—I didn't see it because I was on the ground. I knew we had won, but I didn't see the play until I watched the news that night and heard Tom describe it. That was a thrill.

As a player, as a coach, and as a broadcaster, I've had Tom Kelly call my games, share his stories, play a round of golf, you name it.

When I became the head coach at Oregon State, my team recruited all over the country, but I saved Hawaii and Los Angeles for myself. I ended up in Hawaii once after the team's last game, and USC was in town to play the Rainbow Warriors. I stayed at the Ala Moana Hotel. As I sat under the banyan tree at a circular bar right on the beach, who should show up out of nowhere but the Voice of the Trojans. The mai tais kept flowing.

Later, same place, same bar, at midnight—just Tom and me and two bartenders. Tom asked them, "Do you know the words to 'My Little Grass Shack'?" They didn't. Tom did. And, as you can suspect, that great tenor voice regaled the sudden crowd that had appeared until two in the morning.

Those are times you can't forget.

I've been lucky enough to share a microphone and camera with Tom for 15 years. I've learned a lot about the communication business because of him.

Coach McKay used to have a saying: "If you don't like Tom Kelly, you don't like people." Tom has been my friend and mentor, and I've loved every minute we've been lucky enough to experience together.

Fight on!

—CRAIG FERTIG

USC quarterback, 1962-1964; Passed for a then-single-season school record 1,671 yards, set eight passing records, and won the Davis-Teschke Award for most inspirational player, 1964; USC assistant coach, 1965-1973, 1975; Oregon State head football coach 1976-1979; USC assistant athletic director, 1983-1990; USC Athletic Hall of Fame inductee, 2001; USC football analyst for Fox Sports Net, 1992-2000. Craig Fertig passed away on October 4, 2008.

INTRODUCTION

SINCE THIS BOOK WAS FIRST PUBLISHED, the University of Southern California has become even more of an athletic presence in the NCAA than perhaps the original publication covered.

Recently, many people have talked about the great London Summer Olympics. Did you know that if Olympic athletes associated with USC were somehow formed in their own country, that country might have been as high as sixth in the world in receiving medals—gold, silver and bronze?

Whether you're a Trojan fan or not, the University of Southern California is indeed a force to be reckoned with in almost every college sport. Their football teams of the last few decades have attracted most of the attention, but`—and you can look 'em up—from baseball to volleyball, you'll find individual and team champions whereever you look.

The Trojan "experience" might really have started in 1962, the year I started broadcasting USC football games on radio and later on TV. John McKay's team finished the season undefeated and went on to win the national championship after beating Wisconsin in the Rose Bowl, a post-season game that many still believe may have been one of the greatest ever played. The start of McKay's years at the university ended 15 years later—after four national championships, and two Heisman

Trophy winners—and it set the stage for John Robinson, Larry Smith, Ted Tollner, Robinson again, Pete Carroll and now the present coach, Lane Kiffin. It was the beginning of a 50-year run for a program that, if not a dominating force in college athletics, was certainly a major player in the NCAA.

As the Trojans start 2012 with high expectations and hopes, and even dreams of another Heisman Trophy winner in quarterback Matt Barkley, as well as what could be their 12th national championship, we thought it best to refresh your memory and take you back to where the 50-year saga actually began.

In fact, it really has come full circle for me.

The men who played for that memorable 1962 team were recently honored at a reunion—I was just as honored to be the master of ceremonies for it. This was a group of athletes that may have been best described as "who's he?" when the team was first assembled. There were only 52 men on that roster. But back then, the student population was probably fewer than 10,000. Today, it's more than 35,000, one of the biggest in the country.

It was amazing to see all those who made it back—30 players in all. It was very happy circumstance for them. I did find it kind of strange in that almost every member of that team was a local Southern California resident. Yet, as close as they were as a team, not many had really kept in touch with each other.

They rehashed old memories and caught up on how many marriages and divorces they may have been through. They agreed that while McKay may have been tough on them, he had a remarkable effect on their lives and had done things for them that maybe no other couch could have.

Of course, they talked about the current Trojans team, and they relish the idea that 50 years ago, they did something that this year's squad could do as well.

Pat Haden, the current athletic director, was at the reunion. And it was quite evident that anyone associated with the university realized they were fortunate to have him there to turn to following the NCAA penalties imposed on the Pete Carroll team at the end of Carroll's reign in 2010. Indeed, whether he was invited, cajoled or pulled kicking and screaming into that AD spot, Haden is kind of like Caesar's wife – above reproach. And he's really done a marvelous job.

He spoke to the team about all the problems they had faced, but also about what a remarkable job Lane Kiffin had done stockpiling talent when the NCAA limit on scholarships was in effect for one year. When you look at the talent available for them this year, it's amazing to realize that the program is coming back from NCAA sanctions. It might be a bit more difficult down the line when they're limited in that regard, but in point of fact, this team is in very good shape.

During the recent USC probation, I would attend games and tailgate parties, and enjoyed talking to fans. The dyed-in-the-wool Trojans fans always expect the team to win and to be nationally prominent. When the Trojans don't win, fans are more than a bit upset. That goes back to the days of McKay.

I think fans are also of the opinion that the players today had nothing to do with the problems the university had in the late years of Carroll's coaching regime. But isn't that always the way? As fans see it, the players and coaches today are paying for the sins of people before them that rules and regulations have caught up with. Fans, especially alumni, remain a loyal bunch. They believe that even if you spent just four years at the school, you're always going to be a Trojan for life.

They've helped finance the facilities that have grown dramatically. And they keep coming to every game. The tailgating and lots around the stadium continue to be jammed at 10 in the morning for a 5 p.m. kickoff.

They heard the stories that allege that Carroll left the program for the NFL's riches in Seattle because he knew the NCAA was going to drop the hammer on his program, affecting the team for years to come. I don't know that for a fact, but I do know the new McKay Center that was just completed on campus, which will replace Heritage Hall as the new facility for the football team, was built from dollars raised by Carroll personally. He recruited some $35 million from fans and his close friends to get that facility built. For that effort, there will be a special section named for him in the building.

I really think he left because he didn't think he did as good a job as a pro coach with the New England Patriots and New York Jets and was getting another opportunity (anda great amount of money) to prove he can coach at that level. I don't think Carroll hurt the University of Southern California at all. He recruited great talented athletes, and anyone who knows anything about high-school kids knows they want to play for a winning national program and play on a big stage.

Reggie Bush was one of them. But the Bush saga became a tragedy at the university. He was a magnificent football player. No one questions the things he could do with a football. The fact there were all kinds of allegations about agents and money given to members of his family, I don't know. I'm not privy to any of that. I do find it difficult in this day in age when athletes of Bush's talent are pounced upon by agents in the making, who see him as a gateway to great riches and success. You also have to rely on integrity of the kid and hope he has the right upbringing. Everybody coaching collegiate sports has to deal with that now.

As Carroll left, we were reintroduced to Lane Kiffin. You know that every coach brings baggage with him after going from one place or another. Indeed, Kiffin went from offensive coordinator at USC, to head coach of the Raiders, ended up at the University of Tennessee, and acquired some baggage along the way. But USC officials decided he'd done nothing that could alienate him from the NCAA powers that be. It was a delicate selection with Carroll leaving; everyone knew there would be penalties coming, and that bringing in a man who left Tennessee under some vague circumstances might be a problem as well. Yet in that regard, everything has worked out fine. Kiffin has proven to be a good young coach and excellent recruiter. He's gone out and scoured the country, going to the deep South and Florida and other places to entice some exciting talent to come and play at USC. He brought his dad, Monte, to be the defensive coordinator, though some are concerned that the team needs to improve its tackling. But all in all, their records have been very good, and the fact that USC is now on the threshold of a national title gives credence to the notion that son Lane and dad Monte know how to coach football players.

Bringing Kiffin on board really has proven to be a great hire by the university and could start a new McKay or Carroll or Robinson era. And don't forget, the coaching staff also includes Ed Orgeron—a modern-day Marv Goux, if you will—a magnificent recruiter and a great coach. And don't overlook John Baxter, the special teams coach, who has been absolutely brilliant. I don't think anyone has been able to get a team to turn in blocked punts and field-goal tries like he has. He also developed a series of vital kickers and punters.

Of course, these Trojans have Matt Barkley, a young man anyone would like to have as a son. He's traveled to far-off places in the world, to visit those who live in squalor and poverty, to try to make their lives better. At the same time, there has never been any kind of negative publicity concerning his conduct or deportment.

On the field he obviously knows how to play the quarterback position. And thanks to the efforts of Carroll and Kiffin, he is surrounded by outstanding people to work with. I can't recall the last time I saw Barkley get knocked down while going back to pass. The line takes great care of him. He's had great people to hand the ball to and throw to which works hand in glove in getting the recognition he deserves. When he came back, he said "we had something to prove"—by "we" he meant the players who came through the restrictions and now have come out the other side. So, many years after it was Tailback U., USC has become Quarterback U., and Barkley is in the same mode as a Carson Palmer or Matt Leinart.

And then there are the classic USC match-ups with other teams. At the '62 reunion, of course, they talked of the USC rivalries with UCLA and Notre Dame. Those rivalries remain just as important today as they were in earlier years. People still recall those games chapter and verse. USC has had a run of wins over the Bruins recently, although it goes in cycles. Brothers still play against brothers. That will never change. Just a year ago, we had the McDonald brothers playing against each other, and their father was one of the great USC players of all time. And how is this for a strange turn of events from 2011? USC, with its restrictions, can't win the new Pac-12 South title, but beats the team that will eventually do it, 50-0, in the Trojans' last game of the season, effectively leading to the firing of Bruins coach Rick Neuheisel.

Now Neuheisel has stayed a factor in the Pac-12 with its new TV network, and that in itself is another new twist on how things are changing. Another change is conference expansion, which I don't object to, and Utah and Colorado are welcome additions. They're on the rise. It's just so strange so see so many teams jump places now. You've got teams going from San Francisco to Rhode Island to play teams in their own conference. Can you believe it? San Diego State in the Big East? I can't. There are strange bedfellows in athletics. I can't keep up with it. The Big Ten has 12 teams, and the Big 12 has 10 teams. You can't tell a conference without a map.

One other thing that's happened since the first edition of this book was published is the passing of Craig Fertig, who wrote the original foreward. Craig was a member of that '62 championship team, one of the "to be remembered" performers in USC history. We lost him much too young. The guys at the reunion fondly recalled him on more than one occasion. Craig and I never had an anxious word in the 15 years we worked together in the broadcast booth—probably because, despite my disposition and attitude, I could never find anything to get upset with him about. He was a great human being.

So now, as we complete the circle, we are proud to relive some of the many important moments in Trojan sports history, embrace the present resurgence of the football program, and look forward to the years to come where more tales from the Trojan sidelines are waiting to be told.

Of course, it would be the best of all worlds if Matt Barkley wins the Heisman in 2012, the team wins the national title, and Barkley goes on to have a pro career. What kind of Hollywood ending would that be? But then, this is Hollywood, isn't it? The '62 team thought it was a Hollywood script with what they did, too. Why shouldn't there be another one?

—*TOM KELLY*

TALES FROM THE
USC TROJANS
SIDELINE

1

ASHLAND, IRONWOOD, DULUTH, DES MOINES, PEORIA ...

WHY DID I GET INTO SPORTSCASTING? I wanted to be a rich man's son, but I never made it.

The best way to tell you is to start at the beginning. I'm a Midwesterner by birth. Born in Minneapolis, I attended a couple of high schools in the area. After my father's death, I moved with my mother to Wisconsin. I finished high school there, where my claim to fame as a football player—mostly a defensive end who thought he could be a running back—was having my nose broken by Superior Central High star fullback Bud Grant, the same man who went on to coach the Minnesota Vikings and, really, one of the all-time great athletes to come out of that area.

Grant and I were born just a month apart, and, like him, I went into the service at the end of World War II. By 1948, I had come back out and was working various odd jobs while going to a small college in Northern Wisconsin called Northland.

AN EASY WAY TO MAKE A LIVING

While receiving a degree in English at Northland, I was back to playing football, but I broke my shoulder during a game that year. Our games were on WATW in Ashland, Wisconsin, a 250-watt radio station.

The local announcer, Todd Hogan, needed someone to spot for him. I told him I would, but first I asked him, "What does a spotter do?" He told me I just needed to make sure he knew who was in the game, carrying the ball, throwing, catching, and making the tackles. I thought I could handle that.

In fact, at halftime I said to him, "What an easy way to make a living."

He took some umbrage to it. "You think it's so easy? Why don't you come down and audition for a job?"

I said, "Sure, I can do that."

Two or three of my college friends were working at the station at the time, picking up a few dollars. I happened to be driving a truck and delivering flowers while going to school. And, in those days, the government used to send 52 dollars for 20 weeks to the veterans coming out of that big war. I had just gotten the check and was on my way to the bank to cash it. I had to double-park, but it was a small town and things like that happened. So I went in, cashed the check, came back out, and ran into Todd Hogan. You see, the radio station was right above the bank.

"Thought you were coming to audition," he said to me. "I was looking for you." I thought quickly and said, "I just stopped right now to do it."

So I read some copy. He thought it sounded pretty good, but he couldn't hire me. He said he had to wait for a guy, Wally Huss, to come from the head station, which was 60 miles away in Ironwood, Michigan. That was a 1,000-watt station—really big time. Huss finally came over to Wisconsin and I auditioned for him, too. He said, "Sounds pretty good. C'mon, go to work for us."

CAREER MOVES

So I went to work at WATW in Ashland in 1949 as a morning disc jockey, but I also did high school and college football in addition to basketball for the local teams and my college.

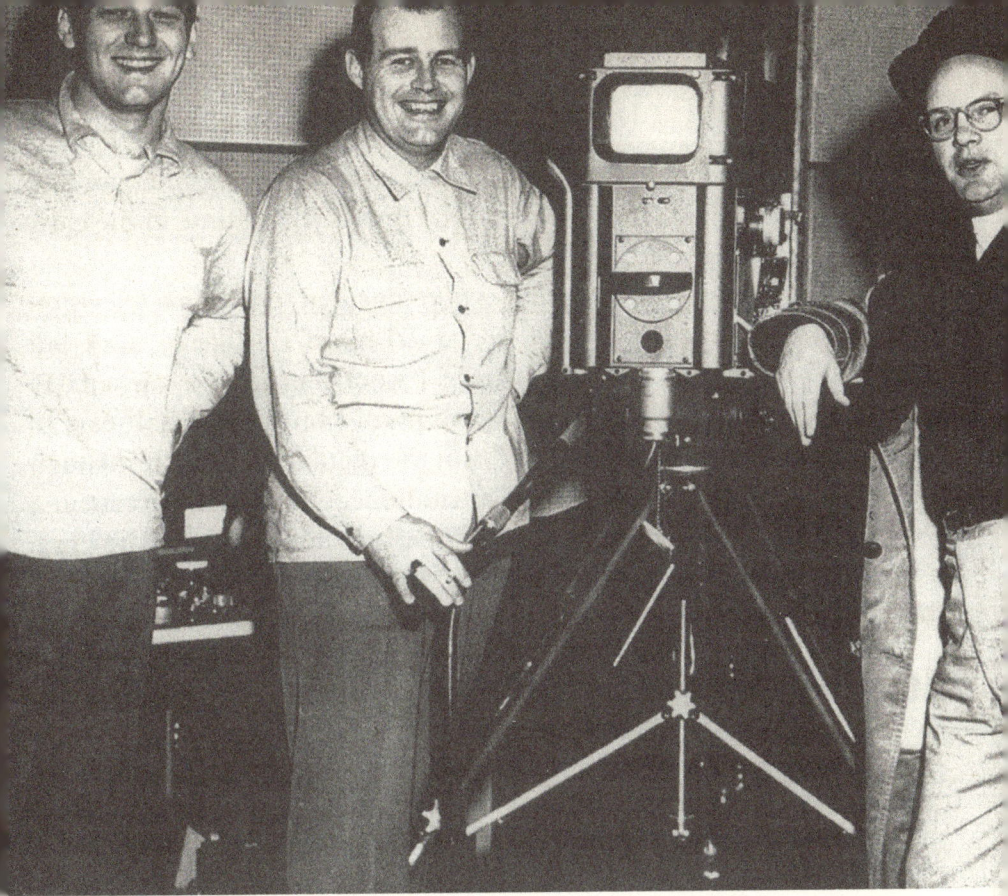

In 1952, at WEBC-TV, Tom Kelly, left, with Mike Flaherty and Norm Gill.
Photo courtesy of Tom Kelly

I never did graduate from Northland because I had too much work ahead of me. It was 1950 and I was moving on Ironwood, Michigan, where I was probably broadcasting 80 high school basketball games and another 40 high school football games a year as sports director.

Two years later, I got a phone call from a guy at Duluth, Minnesota, asking if I'd like to go to work up there. I probably should say that I've been very lucky that I've never had to look for a job while coming through the business. It just seems that I haven't been too successful when I have searched for one in recent years.

While at WEBC in Duluth I added baseball, broadcasting for the Superior Blues and the Duluth Dukes from the old Northern League.

In fact, a kid by the name of Hank Aaron was playing second base and shortstop for the Eau Claire (Wisconsin) Braves at that time in the early '50s. That's how far back this goes.

The man who owned that station then decided to obtain a television grant in Des Moines, Iowa, and he asked me if I'd like to work out there. TV? Why not? So that's where I went. Because it was a UHF station, viewers needed to spend more money on those rabbit ears to get the signal. This was Channel 17, not the regular channels 2 through 13, so we had a tough time getting an audience. We covered everything from car racing to Drake University football and basketball to high school football and basketball. I had a marvelous time in my two years there. But, eventually, the station was forced off the air.

COMING TO PEORIA

Married with two children, I was out of a job. A friend and past employee of mine who had gone to Peoria, Illinois, said the station there, WMBD, wanted a sports announcer to do Bradley basketball, Peoria Caterpillars basketball, and University of Illinois football. He suggested I send a tape to a guy named Chuck Miller, the program director. I didn't have a tape, so I made one.

The legendary Jack Brickhouse, Vince Lloyd, and Jack Quinlan, the Voice of the Cubs in the '50s, had all worked at WMBD. It had a great tradition of announcers. First I called Miller and asked if he had hired anyone yet. The director said he hadn't, but he was just about to make up his mind. "Don't you make any big decisions until you hear my tape," I told him.

I sent him a tape on Monday. He called me back Thursday and asked if I could come in to meet with them. I couldn't make it there until Saturday because I was working at a radio station in Des Moines,

---

Tom Kelly, as he worked at WMBD in Peoria, Illinois. *Photo courtesy of Tom Kelly*

playing records in the morning and reading farm market reports about shoats—those are young pigs, by the way, if you're into that kind of thing.

I drove over to the station and met up with Charles Caley, who they called "Cold Cash" Caley. He was a great man who later turned out to be more like a father than a boss to me. I had to audition for him all over again on Saturday morning before he went out to play golf. He wanted to know if the voice on the tape was really my own and if I could do the job, so I recreated a Drake-Bradley basketball game upstairs and asked the engineer to play a few sound effects and some commercials. Sure enough, I got the job.

It was an interesting time for Bradley basketball, too. This was right after the big point-shaving scandal rocked the program in 1951, when five players admitted to taking bribes. And, back then, the Caterpillars were one of eight teams—including the Bartlesville Phillips 66 Oilers, the Akron Goodyear Wingfoots, the Dayton Air Gems, and the Milwaukee Allen-Bradleys—in the old National Industrial Basketball League, a league made up of mill workers who played for teams that didn't want to join this new organization called the National Basketball Association. If you check back, you'll find that almost every U.S. Olympic team before Pete Newell's 1960 squad was populated with winners from the Amateur Athletic Union tournament, where these teams competed. This goes back to the likes of a UCLA athlete named Sam Balter, who played on the 1932 team. It was great basketball for that area, and the Cats were a very successful team.

So in 1954, I was at the CBS affiliate in Peoria. At the same time, a fellow by the name of Chick Hearn was at the NBC affiliate, and another broadcaster named Bill King, who, shortly after I arrived, left to go to San Francisco and spent a very successful life on a boat doing all the Oakland Raiders, San Francisco Warriors, and Oakland A's games, was working at a competing station.

Hearn and I knew each other. Along with Jack Drees, Hearn and I also worked together on the Illinois high school state basketball tournament telecast. While Hearn left to go to California and Drees left to buy up a couple of radio stations in Alabama, I ended up broadcasting the tournament for 28 years. I'm quite proud of that fact.

At any rate, while doing that, Bradley, and the Caterpillars, we quite often had conflicts between games during the season. The Caterpillars paid the station to do the games; we had to sell Bradley's games. So the Caterpillars took precedence. When those conflicts came up, we needed another announcer to do Bradley games for the old Missouri Valley Conference.

During this time, Jack Buck, who came from Columbus, Ohio, where he went to Ohio State, was in St. Louis fronting the Budweiser bowling team at KMOX in the morning and just waiting for his chance to do St. Louis Cardinals baseball. I'd call Buck—we became great friends—and got him to do those Bradley games.

BECOMING THE VOICE OF THE TROJANS

Now, I've got to tell you, I've become a firm believer in the domino theory. I don't think anything just happens to one person. I think a lot of things happen to a lot of people and truly end up affecting everybody's life. Here's a case in point—win, lose, or draw. Joe Garagiola was doing Cardinals games with Harry Caray then. Joe got a chance to go to NBC in New York to do a game show called *Sale of the Century*. As a result, Jack Buck jumped into the No. 2 seat for Cardinals baseball.

The day Buck got that job, Pat McGuirck, who was the station manager at KNX, the CBS affiliate in Los Angeles, called him. KMOX was an owned-and-operated CBS affiliate. In those days, broadcasters would go from one O-and-O to another, city to city, to find work. McGuirck wanted Buck to come out to L.A. to try out as the new Voice of the USC Trojans because Chick Hearn had just announced he was leaving to do the Lakers.

Tom Kelly, fourth from right, holds a trophy after the Peoria Caterpillars win the 1958 NAAU championship. *Photo courtesy of Tom Kelly*

To think all those things happened within three or four days seems unreal.

Buck's response to McGuirck? "No thanks. I just got the greatest job in the world—something I'd longed for." He, of course, stayed with the Cardinals for more than 40 years and ended up in the Baseball Hall of Fame.

But Buck did tell him, "If you're looking for an announcer, the best one in the world is living in a cornfield 150 miles from here."

And he gave McGuirck my name.

McGuirck called Caley to ask for permission to talk to me, and Caley agreed. McGuirck asked for a tape, but, for all the games I had done, I had no tapes. I had to make another one. Finally, McGuirck asked me to come out for an interview with him and Bob Sutton, the station manager.

I flew out on a Constellation and landed in Burbank. McGuirck met me and put me in the Roosevelt Hotel in Hollywood. The next day, I met Sutton and passed inspection. We also went to the Coliseum to see the Dodgers play the Pirates. I remember Bob Skinner hit one over the left-field wall to beat the Dodgers that night.

I also met Bob Kelley there. And he wanted to punch me in the mouth.

McGuirck had started a series of ads in the *Los Angeles Times* and old Hollywood newspapers that said "Kelly is moving to KNX!" Bob Kelley, who covered the NFL's Rams, was a legend in Los Angeles, and those ads just irritated him so much because everyone who read them thought he was changing jobs. It wasn't until weeks later that he came up to me and apologized for it. He had no idea that I hadn't started the whole thing. And that's aside from the fact that we spelled our last names differently.

I eventually went down to see USC athletic director Jesse Hill, and he wanted to know if I really could do a football game. I said, "You can call my friend, Ray Elliott," the head coach at Illinois. I had his home number in Champaign, dialed it, and gave the phone to Hill, who eventually began laughing. Hill handed me the phone back and Elliott said, "I told him you were the greatest thing since white bread." So I replied, "Well, you didn't want to lie, did you?"

And I got the job.

Now I must tell you, in all honesty, I could recall watching USC and UCLA play football on national television when Red Sanders had his Bruins teams do that serpentine move out of the huddle. But I had no idea which team was which. It didn't take long to learn Howard Jones' history and everything after I saw the many plaques and trophies that day I was interviewed by school administration in the Student Union office. I knew it was a program with true greatness in its history.

So there I was, hired to do USC in 1961.

2

SOUTHERN CALIFORNIA, 1961

IT WAS MY JOB to be the USC football color man for Chick Hearn until he left in November to do the Lakers' broadcast.

In those days, part of the indoctrination for the freshman class coming into USC—which was probably 2,000 strong in 1961—began sometime in August. All students were brought into Bovard Auditorium, where the announcers would do a dog-and-pony show with the head coach, John McKay, and a couple of players who had been warming up right outside on Bovard Field. We'd interviewed the coach, some players—a Pete Beathard, a Bill Nelsen—and a couple of students. We'd then remind the student body that they could see four or five home games on their student activity cards and that the team they were cheering for most wore cardinal and gold. That's an oversimplification, but that's what happened.

I was at the auditorium talking to Jesse Hill when Chick Hearn walked in. I had not seen Hearn since I'd been hired in June. The only time I'd seen him in 1961 was in March, when he came back to do the Illinois state high school basketball tournament telecast. Hearn passed right by me to the other side of the stage. As we were waiting for the show to continue, Jesse looked at me and—I'll never forget it—said, "I thought you knew him."

"Oh, I do," I said. "I know him."

Tom Kelly, left, has dinner with USC athletic director Jesse Hill, who hired him for the Trojans' radio job in 1961. *Photo courtesy of Tom Kelly*

Hearn's part in the program was to introduce Jesse, who would then introduce me. So Hearn introduced Jesse and walked right back out of Bovard. Jesse introduced me and I interviewed McKay, Beathard, Nelsen, and some others.

A WARM WELCOME

We made it to the first game that 1961 season against Georgia Tech on September 22. Only about 36,000 people were at the Coliseum to see a team that had gone 4-6 in John McKay's first season the previous year. I would go on at 7:15 p.m. for the pregame. I was there at 5:30 with copious notes. I had everything I needed to talk about USC football—and they really weren't much to talk about then. So I was prepared.

Hearn walked in around maybe 7:10 and sat down. He didn't say a word to anyone. At 7:15, we were on the air.

"Good evening, welcome to another year of Trojans football. I'm Chick Hearn. Tonight, the Trojans face the Rambling Wreck, the Engineers of Georgia Tech. . . . In a moment, a special announcement to introduce our new color announcer, one of my best friends." And he went to a commercial.

I was flabbergasted.

Now, Hearn and I were never enemies, but best friends? No. Friendly competitors at best. So we came back on and Hearn continued for several moments, literally eulogizing me, telling the folks what a magnificent announcer I was, saying what a great addition I was, etc.

Finally, out of almost total exasperation, I said in a sotto voce voice, "I thought I was doing the game with him."

Hearn really took umbrage with that, and the introduction ended in clenched teeth: "And here's my great friend, Tom Kelly."

Well, USC lost that game 27-7. The next week, the Trojans beat SMU, but only 29,000 fans were at the Coliseum.

HEARN'S DEPARTURE

Hearn never spoke to me until the next-to-last game that year in Pittsburgh—nine games into the season.

It was November 18. USC lost that game 10-9 on a bad call. The day was cold and windy, and I was wrapped up in two or three blankets from the hotel. Don Simonian was the sports information director at USC in those days. And, like every son of an Armenian mother, he could always rely on his mom to send him food. So I was on the air reading a Farmer John commercial script. Simonian had this enormous sausage that his mother had sent him. He threw it out on the table and started to laugh. Hearn saw that, reached over, lit a match, and set the script that I was reading on fire. So I had to read this thing as fast as I could as the copy was burning in front of me. And Simonian started banging that huge sausage on the desk, still laughing.

When I finished the script, Hearn said something rather kind to me: "Nice job!"

McKAY'S ARRIVAL

McKay finished the year 4-5-1—2-1-1 in conference. His team was outscored, and a 10-7 loss to UCLA ended it. He didn't do much better than he had in his first season the year before. No, these were not seasons McKay could be proud of, nor were they what the powers that be at USC wanted.

Dr. Norman Topping was the president. Nick Pappas, a big advocate of McKay, had brought the coach down from Oregon and influenced Topping's decision to hire him. Now McKay's record was 8-10 after two years, and a move was underway to get rid of him.

But McKay, who was smarter than your average black bear, got a sense that his days at SC were numbered. The first thing he did was throw a party for the press, thanking the writers for how well they had treated him and telling them how much he had enjoyed his stay. It was an amazing public relations move. If the press didn't love him before, he was theirs from that moment on, and they belonged to him.

McKay's next bit of business was a trip over to Julie's Restaurant near campus to buy Dr. Topping lunch. McKay really took the play away from the good doctor. He said, "Doctor, I want to talk to you about something," knowing full well the next call would have been from Topping to McKay, asking the coach to come to his office. So they sat in a corner booth that became famous from that point on, if for no other reason than that meeting. They went through several See Throughs, McKay's favorite drink—vodka on the rocks. When Topping made it back to the university, he received a call from the boosters: "Did you fire him?"

From right to left, Tom Kelly poses with Jack Drees and Chick Hearn in 1954 before working on the Illinois State High School basketball tournament. Kelly joined Hearn as part of the USC football broadcasting team in 1961. *Photo courtesy of Tom Kelly*

"No, I hired him, and I'll decide when to fire him. He's still the football coach here. We have to see how he'll do with the players he recruited."

I used to tell people that once I got Hearn out of the booth and once McKay straightened his life out with Topping and the powers that be at the university, we had a great run—starting with an undefeated season in 1962.

3

THE FOOTBALL COACHES

JOHN McKAY (1923-2001)
USC ASSISTANT FOOTBALL COACH: 1959
USC HEAD FOOTBALL COACH: 1960-1975
    127 WINS, 40 LOSSES, 8 TIES
    FOUR NATIONAL CHAMPIONSHIPS (1962, 1967, 1972, 1974)
    5-3 IN THE ROSE BOWL
    8-6-2 VS. NOTRE DAME
    10-5-1 VS. UCLA
NATIONAL COLLEGE FOOTBALL HALL OF FAME: 1988
ROSE BOWL HALL OF FAME: 1991
USC ATHLETIC HALL OF FAME: 1994 (INAUGURAL CLASS)

Sometimes you don't realize you're in the forest until all the trees fade away and you're suddenly standing there with nothing around you. I had no idea then, and, looking back, I'm jolted by the fact that so many things happened in 1962—just one year after John McKay was nearly sent out the door. He had become the toast of the town, having delivered a national championship team and uttering the phrase, "Isn't it wonderful how much smarter I am this year?" That success would continue for the next 16 years. How this Midwest announcer ended up sharing all these moments with USC was just unbelievable.

THE FOOTBALL COACHES

McKay laid an amazing run on Trojans fans, elevating West Coast football and bringing the program to a level of prominence even with Notre Dame, Alabama, and all the other great ones, and, in most cases, placing USC at the forefront of college football.

How did it happen? Part of the secret to his success, I believe, was the fact that he went out and recruited outstanding athletes, not just outstanding players. Many of them were not big physically, but just very talented. For example, Hal Bedsole, who went to Reseda High and Pierce Junior College, was an outstanding quarterback, but McKay turned him into one of the most legendary wide receivers in the history of SC football. Tom Lupo went from quarterback at Birmingham High to defensive end and place kicker at USC. Pete Beathard was a great athlete from El Segundo who could have played any position. He was the quarterback. He was also an outstanding baseball player who wanted to play for Rod Dedeaux's national championship teams, but McKay asked him to stick with football. Bill Nelsen, a quarterback out of Cerritos Junior College, wasn't very big, but neither were many of USC's offensive linemen.

The other part of McKay's success was in how he dealt with the media. I got my first taste of it back in '61—third game of the season, early October. USC had just lost 35-34 in a back-and-forth game at Iowa. The Trojans scored last with 48 seconds left. McKay had a chance to win the game, but the two-point conversion failed.

The football writers used to meet at the Sheraton Downtown. After that game, one of the scribes asked McKay, "Did you ever consider going for a tie?"

McKay, who could freeze you with a look while tapping on that cigar, always liked to use the phrase "playing for a tie was like kissing your sister." In this case, he went further: "Son, in case you hadn't noticed, the damn game was tied when we kicked off. That's why we played the game, to break the tie."

But then I saw him soften. Saying something like that could have come back to haunt him in the press, so he added, "Yes, I might have

for a moment, but . . . " Well, the rest of the press thought one of their fellows had been pretty well had and enjoyed it. But that's how McKay was. His one-liners made us laugh, and he won over the local media right away.

Now, understand, we didn't always see eye to eye, either. I'm sure he thought I didn't know a football from a tennis racket, but my admiration for him never wavered.

Back in the early '60s when George Putnam was the big local news anchor, I'd do a show for KTTV Channel 11. We'd bring a camera down to the local press gathering and tape a segment—maybe four minutes long—in which I'd interview McKay about last Saturday's game. Then we'd re-run his comments over the tape and talk about the game coming up.

I remember the game that previous Saturday had one of those typical McKay plays: USC is deep in the other team's territory on third down and maybe 5 to go when McKay calls a time out. He stands there on the sidelines, puts his finger to his lips, and, with the quarterback standing next to him for what seemed to be an interminable length of time, he finally says something, sends the quarterback back on to the field, and is eventually called for a delay-of-game penalty. In total frustration on the broadcast, I finally said something about how many times we'd seen this delay-of-game penalty called.

McKay used to have an expression for everyone—and most of them you can't repeat. But for the announcer, it was "bastard." After every game, he'd ask one of his assistant coaches, "What did that bastard say about me?" And they'd have to tell him what they'd heard me say.

So McKay walks into this press lunch on a Monday and the first thing he says to me is, "I thought you and I were pals." Several writers hear him say this as we take the discussion out to the hallway, and they

---

Tom Kelly, left, and John McKay pose at the USC practice field in the 1970s.
Photo courtesy of Tom Kelly

get their notepads out because they think they'll get a story out of the coach ripping the broadcaster.

"What is this bull you're giving me about the delay-of-game penalties?" McKay asked me.

I stood there for the longest minute, not knowing what to do. "If I'm wrong, I'll apologize," I finally said.

He gave me another one of those looks that could freeze you. "OK, Tommy, let's do this interview," he said, and that was the end of the conversation. I had finally won a point.

From his demeanor on the sidelines, you always knew McKay was a deep thinker and an intense coach, but that fact really hit home for me after a game in 1964. Remember, McKay wins a national title in '62, finishes '63 with a 7-3 mark, and, going back to last season, he's won seven of his last eight before his team, ranked second in the nation, is hit with a 17-7 loss at East Lansing, Michigan. Duffy Daugherty, the Michigan State coach, had a stable full of these great little pony backs who could tear you apart.

I did the postgame show and then went down to the team plane, where we would leave East Lansing for Chicago, stop in Omaha for gas, and then get home to L.A. I'm looking for a place to sit on the plane, and Dave Levy, one of the assistant coaches, points to the two empty seats in the front. I said, "No, Coach McKay will be sitting there."

Dave said, "And you're sitting right there next to him. None of the coaches are going to sit next to him after that game."

So McKay sat down. I'd never seen him madder or more irate. He was not so much ashamed as embarrassed over what had happened. Before the door even closed, he started talking to me about the game as if I was a player or a coach. As we were landing, I finally said, "John, I just broadcast the games."

But he went right by that remark. He said, "I promise, Tommy, we'll never be small again."

That loss really tore him up. Competing against Big Ten schools with offensive guards like one of USC's captains, Bill Fisk, who may have been good but wasn't an enormous man at 6 feet and 220 pounds, inspired McKay from then on to find big bodies to take care of whoever was in the game. Two weeks later, USC lost 17-0 at Ohio State, but they handed Notre Dame a legendary 20-17 defeat at home in the last game of the season.

I think back on all those days at Julie's, where McKay would visit with his fellow coaches. Nothing there could or should be repeated. He was the king of the walk. If you were a daily newspaper columnist stuck for a story, there was a given period of time when you could just give McKay a call and ask him what was going on. Your editor would tell you what a great job you did and McKay would have you in his pocket for life. If he had trouble with the team or with the university, it was only human nature to ease up on the man for all he'd done for you. McKay was always well liked because he was honest. And it's hard to argue against success.

McKay would take me to the Rose Bowl so many times. Is there any need to tell you how much I loved those years? But all the success McKay had, especially from 1972 on, led to a very strange ending in 1975. Here was a man with team records of 12-0, 9-2-1, and 10-1-1. In '75, his team was 7-0 going into a game at Cal. Maybe he just needed a new challenge.

McKay had some problems with those in power at the university, though he'd never say what they were. Just prior to the '75 season, he almost took an NFL job with the Los Angeles Rams, but for one reason or another turned it down. At USC, he was the be-all and end-all. Fifteen years of great football later, the team was still a major item. I suppose he felt he deserved something more, but I don't think McKay was ready for a pro coaching job, where you're at the whim of what you can't control. As a college coach, you give the guy you want a scholarship. In the NFL, you're stuck with the people you draft, even if you don't want them. Your career rises and falls with what the team does. I think that may have been part of the reason why he didn't go to the Rams.

But by 1975, McKay's problems with the university hierarchy didn't improve. He won seven games: Duke, Oregon State, Purdue, Iowa, Washington State, Oregon, and a 24-17 victory at Notre Dame—the last time he'd go to South Bend to coach against the Irish. With a record of 7-0, the team was ranked third in the nation. But between the time they made it home and the time they went up to Berkeley to face a Bears team led by Chuck Muncie a week later, something happened.

To show how bitter he was about everything, McKay waited until he stepped off the plane in Oakland before he announced he was leaving. Think of what he could have done with a press conference in Los Angeles.

McKay had accepted the positions of head coach and general manager of the Tampa Bay Buccaneers, an expansion team. As for USC, McKay had, for the most part, just packed it in. And the team fell flat at Cal, losing 28-14. Next, they came home and lost to Stanford 13-10 with no time left. They were defeated 8-7 by Washington State in the closing minutes at Pullman and then lost to UCLA 25-22, falling out of the Top 20 rankings. Marv Goux, who basically coached the team the rest of the year, refused to let McKay go out with a loss, leading USC to a victory over Texas A&M in the Liberty Bowl.

With McKay's departure, the natural assumption was that Dave Levy or Goux would be given the job and the beat would go on. I think Levy was red-flagged because of his association with UCLA, having played for Red Sanders back in the '50s. Goux might have been painted with a bad brush—if McKay recommended him, the school's powers that be ruled him out. At that point, even if McKay had said, "Let Tom Kelly coach the team," the university would have said no.

Back in the late '80s, I was the executive producer of a series on the history of USC football. Pat McClenahan, the producer and editor of our production company, joined me on a trip to Tampa, Florida, to interview McKay. We arrived at John's place, met him and his wife, Corky, and spoke in the atrium about how we would like to do interviews in an old antebellum at his house. McKay wanted to know our schedule, but he also wanted to know if I'd brought my golf clubs.

Pat and I had played the previous day at Baltusrol Golf Club in New Jersey. "What's your handicap?" McKay asked. I told him I was a 9.

He asked his son, Rich, for his handicap. Richie said he was an 11. He asked his son-in-law, Bob. He said he was also a 9. "Well, I'm a 14," McKay says. "Tomorrow, you and I will play together against Richie and Bob out at Avila." We decide to play this match for $100.

I could play reasonably well back then; I wouldn't embarrass anyone. But every time we'd tee off, Richie's ball would land next to mine and Bob's would drop about 20 yards in front of it. I'm thinking, "These guys are a 9 and an 11? No matter how good I hit it, they're in front of me!"

We get to the 17th hole, a par-5. Richie is maybe 30 yards in front of me. I hit my second shot to the front edge of the green, but Richie's second shot makes it to the back of the green. I putt it six inches to the cup and they let me pick it up for a birdie. Richie chips and almost knocks it in.

"How do we stand?" McKay asks me before the last hole.

"Well, we're one down," I tell him, still pretty confounded.

The 18th is a short par-4. McKay decides it's time to press 'em.

He steps up and knocks it 30 feet off into the area where the no-shoulders people live, so we've lost that tee shot. The three of us left hit into the fairway and then to the green. I miss my birdie but make par. They make their routine pars.

I'm trying to settle the bet with Bob and let Richie and his dad settle their bet inside the clubhouse. As we're ordering a round of drinks, McKay asks how we ended up. I have to tell him we've lost, and I reach into my pocket to pay up.

McKay says, "Tommy, you're the dumbest SOB I've ever known. Bob here played on the PGA Tour out of Florida State. Richie is the club champion here and was the captain of the golf team at Princeton."

Good God, no wonder we lost.

"Didn't you notice they were hitting it past you on every hole?" McKay asked. "You don't owe anybody anything."

It was all just a big gag.

I may be wrong, but for him to have thought up that entire charade and gone out of his way to put me in a game with his son and son-in-law, I think he must have liked me. I've hung my hat on the fact that he thought enough of me to set up that whole routine the night before.

I know that USC finally plans to honor him this year by renaming the Coliseum McKay Field. He deserves it. Who else has had a greater record? I realize that his sons scattered his ashes along the field's sidelines, but I wasn't aware that the Trojans haven't lost a home game since they did so. Are you telling me he's looking down on us? I don't want to elevate him to that high of a power; he was quite human, as many of us are.

Looking back, he was the type of guy who was very much tuned in to a situation and quick to adapt to it. McKay also dealt with the rule that stated if a player substituted in, he couldn't come out until that quarter was over. So McKay came up with a red, gold, and green team. One would play defense best. Another was strictly an offensive team. The last group could do both. It was an innovative move no one really picked up right away.

After McKay's first two losing seasons, were high school kids rushing to go to USC? The charm and mystique have lured some, but if recruited by an Ohio State or even a Cal or Stanford, a local Southern California kid may have left. But somehow, McKay remained a great recruiter on a national level. You bring a kid in back in 1963 or even in 2007 and his first reaction will be, "Do we have games on TV? Who do we play? Will I start?" McKay gave everyone that opportunity. First he captured the media attention of a great market on TV. He then elevated the conference to a national level. He brought a level of respect to USC; no visiting team would have a walk in the park.

It's hard to say when I last saw John—probably at the Eisenhower Medical Center out in Palm Springs. We spent an afternoon downtown with Corky. I know that one of the proudest moments of my life was being invited to represent the media at his memorial service at Bovard Auditorium. I probably didn't deserve it. Someone like Bud Furillo or Loel Schrader, two of the media writers who'd known McKay, was probably more deserving, but what a privilege. I was quite honored.

JOHN ROBINSON
USC ASSISTANT COACH: 1972-1974
USC HEAD FOOTBALL COACH: 1976-1982, 1993-1997
    104 WINS, 35 LOSSES, 4 TIES
    4-0 IN THE ROSE BOWL
    8-3-1 VS. NOTRE DAME
    5-7 VS. UCLA
ROSE BOWL HALL OF FAME: 2003

One of the smartest moves John Robinson made after the 1974 season was becoming an assistant coach for his boyhood friend, John Madden, with the Oakland Raiders. I think he knew a change was coming at USC that concerned John McKay, so it was wise of Robinson to go away. When he came back, he came back as the man who had everything going for him.

He had been on McKay's staff, knew the personnel, and was in step with all that was going on. He saw the opportunity and everything that came with it, and he anticipated the best way to take the job. I know his interview with President Hubbard was a simple phone call. He was in. I can't think of anyone else who was offered the job. Robinson's appointment may have been a foregone conclusion.

For Robinson, success bred more success. First, he had inherited great talent. He also had Marv Goux, who led him to two more Heisman Trophy winners—Charlie White and Marcus Allen—plus Paul McDonald, Ricky Bell, and Vince Evans. He began his career with a loss at Missouri. To this day, no one can tell you how that 46-25 butt-kicking against the country's eighth-ranked team happened. But Robinson came back to win 11 in a row, including that 14-6 win over Bo Schembechler and Michigan at the Rose Bowl, and finish the year ranked second—one spot ahead of the Wolverines and behind Pittsburgh.

That was the start of another incredible run. Robinson may have sent 30 players to the pros from '78 to '81. He had an amazingly gifted group of athletes—White, Allen, Ronnie Lott, Brad Budde, Anthony Munoz, George Achica, Dennis Smith, Bruce Matthews, Chip Banks, Roy Foster, Keith Van Horne, Jack Del Rio, Don Mosebar, Joey Browner—who played every bit as well as they were advertised.

To put things in the proper context, when I look at how Robinson coached his teams, I compare him to Pete Carroll. But Robinson, I believe, had a better rapport with successful athletes. There have been other great coaches who were nice and able to get along well with their players, but those players were either ordinary or unable to take the team to a national title. Robinson had great players. Some may have had ego problems, but those were never displayed. Not only were his players going to win, but they were going to play their hearts out for him.

Robinson never wore a headset on the sidelines and he was always around to give each player a big handshake and pat on the back. By comparison, McKay was rather businesslike. You played, you did what you were expected to do, and you came back to the bench. Only on very rare occasions would he personally grab a player and give him some sort of a hug. He may have said something or given a nod, a smile, or a wave, but he was nothing like Robinson. Even after Robinson left to coach the Rams and UNLV, you still saw him with his arms around players and never with a finger in their faces. The magnificent coach's success, which originated with great players, ended with a 26-10 loss at the Fiesta Bowl against Penn State on New Year's Day. Robinson left after the next season, 1982, when the team was banned from postseason bowl games because of an NCAA penalty.

THE FOOTBALL COACHES

Think back to that win over Notre Dame on November 30, 1996, at the Coliseum. It was the last game of a season that had its ups and downs. The unranked Trojans, who'd lost three in a row—including that 48-41 game at the Rose Bowl against UCLA in two overtimes the week before—pulled out a 27-20 overtime victory against the 10th-ranked Irish when linebacker Mark Cusano knocked down a pass on fourth down. Remember, USC hadn't beaten Notre Dame since 1982, Robinson's last year in his first coaching stint at USC.

When the contest was over, I received word from our game director that I had to go to the dressing room to interview Robinson. The cameraman and I fought through the crowd to get down there. John finally came out of the locker room with sweat pouring down his face and his hair all askew. And, for whatever reason, he put his arm around me as the camera turned on and he gave me a kiss on the cheek.

I looked at him and then into the camera and said, "Oh, that's nice, but we won't pick out furniture until Monday. Congratulations."

Maybe Robinson was comfortable doing that to me because he'd been my broadcast partner for a couple of seasons between the time he left the Rams and returned to the USC sidelines in 1993. Some fans may have thought Robinson was angling for the head coaching job again as we did games, watching Larry Smith pull the team through some tough times. After a 3-8 season in '91, Smith's team posted losses against UCLA, Notre Dame, and Fresno State in the Freedom Bowl in Anaheim to finish 6-5-1.

Robinson and I broadcast that game against Notre Dame at the Coliseum. Trailing by eight with three minutes left, USC had the ball near midfield. They ran a play. The clock, which had already ticked down to 2:10, was still moving. They ran another play. Only 1:30 was left. Smith finally called a time out. He had three timeouts to use when the series started.

I finally turned to John and said, "He had three timeouts a few minutes ago, but now it's down to 1:10 and he's still got two left. Is he saving them as a Christmas present to give to someone?"

Robinson didn't say anything. Finally, we went to a commercial and Robinson said to me, "Boy you were tough on him."

Well, USC could have called a timeout, figured out a couple of plays to run, and then called another timeout.

"Would you have said that about me if I was down there coaching?" Robinson asked.

"If you did that," I replied, "you bet I would." And that was the end of that conversation.

I can't put words in his mouth, but I think the fact that Robinson came back to coach was a fait accompli. He was a good broadcaster with an admirable trait—and that was letting me, an old loudmouth, say whatever it was he might have wanted to say himself.

When Robinson took over in 1976, he may have inherited a team rich in talent. But why this man isn't in the USC Hall of Fame remains a mystery to me this day.

MARV GOUX (1933-2002)
USC LINEBACKER/CENTER: 1952, 1954-1955
USC ASSISTANT FOOTBALL COACH: 1957-1982
    COACHED ON FIVE NATIONAL CHAMPIONSHIP TEAMS
    COACHED ON 11 ROSE BOWL TEAMS
USC ATHLETIC HALL OF FAME: 1994 (INAUGURAL CLASS)
ROSE BOWL HALL OF FAME: 2000

I never saw Marv Goux without a shirt, coat, and tie. I never saw him without the buzz cut that reflected his Marine background. In many ways, he was a Marine drill sergeant who had great respect for his players. He challenged everyone he coached on the practice field. He got down on the line with the team. He could do more one-armed push-ups than anyone I'd ever seen, even though his back had been operated on a couple of times.

Years ago, when I first started doing games, the coaches worked down in the cellar of Bovard Auditorium, which was purported to be a locker room. They would get everyone in there—jamming it full with 60, 70, 80 players—until it was hotter than the hots of Hell. Goux would then enter and start talking about the next opponent. By the time he'd get through with you and all the accoutrements in the room, you'd just want to kill somebody. That was Goux's specialty, and nobody did it better. If you had any doubt that you would win, he'd dispel it. Even I was fired up.

And you know he was best at motivating the teams for the USC-Notre Dame game. When we had the chance to interview him for the USC history video project, he was an assistant with John Robinson and the Rams and had an office out in Orange, California. He was rummaging through his desk when he found an old program from a USC-Notre Dame game that showed two gigantic linemen, each holding a helmet with tape and mud and dirt all over them. Cut and bleeding, they just stood there looking at each other. And Goux, with tears in his eyes, lowered his voice and said, "That's what that game is about."

When McKay left, people naturally assumed that Goux would replace him. I think he wanted to be a head coach, but in all honesty, I don't think he had the temperament to be one. He was best suited as an assistant, and was one of McKay's best.

A head coach must deal with the details, focusing on all the extra stuff that needs to be done. He sells his program to the press while the guys in the trenches are hired as real coaches. That was Goux's calling. He stayed at the university when Robinson took over and eventually went with him to the Rams. I don't know if Goux wanted to go to Tampa Bay to join McKay. His heart was at USC and he fit his role to a T.

His biggest coup may have been landing O.J. Simpson at a time when Simpson had nearly made up his mind to go elsewhere. Simpson had just finished a fine freshman season at San Francisco Community College and Al Saroni, a big money donor from the Zellerbach family, had given him a job up in the Bay Area. Simpson's first wife, Marguerite, called Goux, who was at a party in Orange County,

From left to right, John Robinson, John McKay, Tom Kelly, 1959 head coach Don Clark, and Marv Goux pose together at a function in the 1970s. *Photo courtesy of Tom Kelly*

California, and said, "You'd better get up here because there's a coach from Utah State who's driving down to get him. I've been told to pack his bags."

Goux said, "Tell him not to move, I'll be there." Goux got on a plane and, within an hour, was at Simpson's house in the Potrero Heights area of San Francisco, not too far from Candlestick Park.

The story goes that Goux walked in and Simpson wanted to know what he was doing there. "I came to help you pack," said Goux. "I'm here to help you throw your life away. You can go to Utah State, but I guarantee no one will ever know your name again. If you get your grades straight and come to USC, I guarantee you'll be a household name the rest of your life." Goux really laid it on him, chewing him out from one end to the other. When the Utah State coach arrived, Simpson said, "I'm not going with you." He forever thanked Goux for talking him into staying with USC.

Goux's other amazing recruiting story relates to the time he was after Tim Rossovich, the 6-foot-5 defensive end from St. Francis High in Mountain View, California. Here was a guy who'd eat light bulbs and chew razor blades. Everyone was talking about him. On a day Goux was up there to recruit Rossovich, Stanford head coach John Ralston went to see him, too. So they both arrived at the house as Rossovich's father was making a big kettle of soup. It was some sort of bullion, but floating around in the enormous pot were a bunch of fish eyes.

The story goes, as Goux told me, that Rossovich's father said to Ralston, "You'll stay and have lunch."

Ralston looked into that pot and said, "No, I've got important business in the city, I've got to go."

So the father turned to Goux and said, "You'll stay?"

And Goux said, "You bet. And I'll have some of that," pointing to the fish floating around.

Now, whether or not Goux was guilty of scalping tickets in the early '80s, the program was put on two years NCAA probation. Shame on the university if they allowed Goux to do so. But USC extolled the virtues of Marv Goux, and rightfully so. They could hang a picture of him next to Tommy Trojan and no one would object.

In the hearts and minds of anyone who has spent any time with the program over the past 40 years, Goux epitomized that spirit the university likes to recognize. It is too bad he was the victim of a scandal that became a national joke, as though someone at 30th and Figueroa invented the idea of providing tickets for players.

Goux will forever be a cherished Trojan. To this day, years after he's left us, people still talk about the 5-foot-10, 185-pound linebacker out of Santa Barbara, California. The coaches still give out the Marv Goux Award to the Trojan who has the best performance in the game against

UCLA. And his plaque still hangs at the entrance of the practice field, designating it Goux's Gate. No other coach remained an assistant for any head coach as long as he did. He was unbelievable.

CRAIG FERTIG
USC ASSISTANT FOOTBALL COACH: 1965-1973, 1975

One of my favorite Craig Fertig stories is the one he tells about the time Alabama coach Bear Bryant came out to Pepperdine to attend a coaching clinic. John McKay told his assistant coach, "You pick Bryant up at the Miramar Hotel in Santa Monica, take care of him, and see that everything's first class." Fertig made it to the hotel at a quarter to seven, called the room, woke the Bear up, and had a Bloody Mary or two with him. Then they drove out to Pepperdine and walked into the clinic. After Bryant was introduced, he collapsed. Paramedics had to take him to the hospital.

Fertig was thinking, "Well, if I live, I'll never be able to explain to Coach McKay what happened to his best friend while he was in my charge." Fertig finally called McKay, who came down to the hospital. The doctor told him that Bryant would be OK, but they needed to keep him a couple of days.

"By the way," the doctor asked McKay, "where has this patient been the last week or so?"

"Well, he's been with me in Palm Springs. Why?"

"Because," the doctor said, "he's suffering from acute alcohol poisoning."

With that, Fertig had to smile. McKay nodded and walked out the door.

THE FOOTBALL COACHES

DAVE LEVY
USC ASSISTANT FOOTBALL COACH: 1960-1975

If Marv Goux was called "The Killer," then Dave Levy was "The Range Bull." The two were inseparable.

Though never examined or verified, it was my thought that Dave Levy should have been the man to replace John McKay as head coach in 1976. Apparently, it wasn't going happen. Levy had had great national success as an offensive lineman for Red Sanders at UCLA in 1952 and '53. Maybe he was still regarded as the guy who went to UCLA, although it had been years since his playing days. He didn't have any clout with the powers that be at USC and was not considered for the position.

Now helping the Harvard-Westlake High School program out in the Valley, Levy is to this day a brilliant football mind who has shown his great ability on both offense and defense. He understands all aspects of the game. Not only was Levy McKay's top assistant, but he also made a great assistant for Tom Prothro and Don Coryell with the San Diego Chargers.

TED TOLLNER
USC ASSISTANT COACH: 1982
USC HEAD FOOTBALL COACH: 1983-1986
- 26 WINS, 20 LOSSES, 1 TIE
- 1-0 IN THE ROSE BOWL
- 0-4 VS. NOTRE DAME
- 1-3 VS. UCLA

Ted Tollner may have been victimized by the fact that, when John Robinson left for the Los Angeles Rams, he took with him nearly everyone off that Trojans coaching staff, including Marv Goux. And it was a great staff.

The closet was bare, though I do not want to denigrate the players who contributed after 1981. Tollner had outstanding players, not the least of whom was Rodney Peete, who came very close to winning the Heisman Trophy. The fact that Tollner brought a player like Mark Carrier to USC is testament to his recruiting skills as well.

Tollner was well liked and a fine coach, but he fell into a tough situation and had to make do. He also had to deal with probation.

I once remember sitting with Tollner and his wife, Barbara, at Julie's as the press swarmed around one day. Ted wasn't having the success he really wanted, and Barbara asked me in confidence, "Do they like him?"

"They love him," I told her. "He's a nice man. They like him because of all that."

"What happens if he's not successful?" she asked.

"They'll still write nice things about him because they like him and he's been fair."

Tollner was never antagonistic, and it's great that he's still coaching elsewhere.

LARRY SMITH
USC HEAD FOOTBALL COACH: 1987-1992
    44 WINS, 25 LOSSES, 3 TIES
    1-2 IN THE ROSE BOWL
    0-6 VS. NOTRE DAME
    3-2-1 VS. UCLA

I admired Larry Smith and thought he was a very nice man, but I felt he didn't understand that the Los Angeles market wasn't like what he'd come from before as the coach of the University of Arizona back in Tucson. L.A. is so much bigger—the media numbers alone are overwhelming. When you say something, thousands, not just hundreds, read it. That's a quantum leap from Tucson. You'd have a press conference on a Tuesday, and 10 to 15 guys from the Inland Empire to San Diego would be there. That may have caught up with him.

Smith also did some things that I felt were rather strange. For example, junior Mazio Royster had run for more than 1,000 yards and had a great Hancock Bowl performance (with a game-high 125 yards on 32 carries, he was only the second player to break 100 yards on the ground against Michigan State that season). But when Smith was asked who'd start at running back the next year, he said he hadn't made up his mind yet. To me, Royster was never the problem, and that '91 team finished 3-8, losing their last six.

This isn't to say Smith didn't have some great years. He went to the Rose Bowl his first three seasons. And, may I tell you, of all the coaches who took me along to the Rose Bowl, Larry Smith was the only one who gave me a Rose Bowl ring.

PETE CARROLL
USC HEAD FOOTBALL COACH: 2001-PRESENT
    65 WINS, 11 LOSSES
    TWO NATIONAL CHAMPIONSHIPS (2003, 2004)
    2-1 IN THE ROSE BOWL
    1-0 IN THE ORANGE BOWL
    5-1 VS. NOTRE DAME
    5-1 VS. UCLA

Though I did the Trojans coaches show every week while at Fox Sports Net two years back, I haven't gotten to know Pete Carroll all that well. But from where I sit, I think he embodies the best of John McKay and John Robinson, two great coaches of the modern era. USC is indeed fortunate to have him.

Carroll can obviously coach. And, as a recruiter, he has a great sense of talent. Because of today's vast scouting systems and publications, it's easy to spot the best players in Louisiana, Carolina, or even Lost Overshoe, Nevada. But Carroll knows how to hook them.

The head coach tells recruits, "If I didn't think you couldn't start for me, I wouldn't be in your living room. If you don't want that kind of a challenge, stay home and play where you want. But I'm all in favor of you winning a starting spot." It is one of Carroll's greatest attributes.

He has a great rapport with today's kids, even star quarterbacks, running backs and receivers who now have to consider all the money they would earn in the NFL. The turnover, as Carroll has found, is tremendous, and a player's life expectancy in the NFL is short. If he can walk away without a limp and a cane, he's the exception. So athletes are tempted to leap to the NFL. I have no argument with kids who go on. Tearing up a knee for Sidewash U. is great, but you'll have a limp when you try to make a living.

What Carroll's doing now can be compared to what McKay and Robinson did when they started their USC coaching careers—all three could put the team on the front page of the paper. In the '60s or '70s, when a player like Gary Jeter out of Cleveland or Richard Wood out of New Jersey decided to come to USC, it was because they saw the Trojans on TV. Once they were contacted, they jumped at the chance. Carroll has that same kind of lure.

When you watch him on the sidelines, he looks 30 years younger than he is, just like one of the players. The ups are great, the downs drive him crazy, and he laughs alongside his team. Carroll now knows how to deal with the media, too, because he's currently working from a place of strength. That first year he was here, he produced a 6-6 team with a loss in the Las Vegas Bowl. He's really come a long way in a short time. People now know USC isn't going to lose to a Utah or a North Carolina or a Fresno State. Those are wake-up calls for universities that want to be a cut above the rest.

Carroll's national championships are especially impressive because it is so difficult to win them today. Many teams don't even get to play for the championship, like Boise State, which last year got caught in that BCS mess. We're no longer even sure the two best teams meet. Although you may have the best squad, you may never get the chance to claim a national title. If you're lucky enough to get to the championship, it's a major coup.

THE FOOTBALL COACHES

It's much tougher to sneak up on anyone, too. Every recruit knows every big-time coach, and every coach knows every recruit. McKay and Robinson probably didn't have to deal with that in their heydays. Then, it all boiled down to only four or five teams fighting for a national championship every year. USC had fewer opponents to conquer, and the bowl system was different. If your record proved worthy, you were accepted to be the best.

To be honest, when Carroll first accepted the job with USC, I didn't know what would happen. He didn't start out any better than Paul Hackett, but he found the magic. Think about how tough it is to be the center of attention in this media market now. All you have to do is make one mistake before you go from the best to "Who's he?" As everyone in the show business world knows, it's true that you may only get 15 minutes of fame in this town. You can come and go in a flash.

Carroll came in and didn't have a great year. Think about what happened to McKay after his first two years. You couldn't have found a Trojans fan who'd say he was going to win a national championship in '62. Carroll is similar to McKay in that way. I believe they differ in the way they handle the media. Carroll has a kind of hesitancy when fielding endless questions, whereas McKay confronted and took over the media.

Today, Carroll faces a legacy: every time he puts a team on the field, that team is expected to win. I can't imagine the kind of pressure that's been put on his staff and the program to perform up to the expectations of not just every Trojans fan, but every person who looks at the entire national scene. Beating someone 7-6 is as good as a loss. Holding UCLA to 13 points in a USC defeat is a shame on somebody. I don't know if McKay felt that kind of burden before a string of Rose Bowls in the mid-'60s.

We'll see how the head coach reacts to the pressure. I'm a big Carroll fan.

4

OTHER USC NOTABLES

ROD DEDEAUX (1914-2006)
USC HEAD BASEBALL COACH: 1942-1986
  1,332 WINS, 571 LOSSES, 11 TIES
  11 COLLEGE WORLD SERIES TITLES (1958, 1961, 1963, 1968, 1970-1974, 1978)
  28 CONFERENCE TITLES
U.S. OLYMPIC BASEBALL COACH: 1984
USC ATHLETIC HALL OF FAME: 1994 (INAUGURAL CLASS)
COLLEGE BASEBALL HALL OF FAME: 2006 (INAUGURAL CLASS)

You won't believe how I first became aware of Rod Dedeaux. Remember, the Student Union building used to have a long hallway full of cubbyholes in 1961. I walked into one office, and Forrest Twogood, the basketball coach, was with one of his assistants, Danny Rogers. I saw this other desk back in the corner just covered with dust and piled high with 16-millimeter film of the basketball team.

"Whose desk is that?" I asked.

"That's our baseball coach," Twogood said.

"He doesn't come in here often, does he?" I asked.

"Doesn't have to," said Twogood. "He's a millionaire and he's the most successful coach in the world."

OTHER USC NOTABLES

Dedeaux had already won a couple of national championships and already owned a trucking company, Dart Transportation, a multimillion-dollar endeavor he founded in 1938. He had the best of all possible worlds.

I think Dedeaux had to be every bit to college baseball what John Wooden was to college basketball. When you think about the success John McKay had on the football field in the early '70s—a record of 31-3-2 at one point and three straight Rose Bowls—consider Dedeaux, who won six national championships in seven years between 1968 and 1974.

Dedeaux and McKay, the athletic director at that time, were kindred spirits—larger-than-life figures in a larger-than-life period in USC history. It doesn't get much better than that.

I did broadcast a number of Dedeaux's baseball games, but not as many as I could have. Dedeaux, who began as a player at USC and later coached with Sam Barry, was one of the most sacred cows the university had ever produced among its coaches, and deservedly so.

Dedeaux will tell you he won 12 national championships, even though the record books say 11. He told me so during a broadcast. After we had set up the tape for an interview once, I began, "Welcome to Dedeaux Field, I'm Tom Kelly, and next to me is the nonpareil of baseball coaches, Rod Dedeaux, with 11 national championships . . ."

He stopped me right there.

"Twelve," he said.

I told the cameraman to hold it just a second.

I thought I'd done my due diligence and checked all the facts. The record books said 11.

"Twelve," he said again. "And here's the ring to prove it."

He showed me a ring that represented the 1960 USC baseball team.

"It was one of the best teams I ever coached," he said.

At that time, the Amateur Athletic Union was breaking up, and all kinds of people in the Pac-8 were blowing the whistle on other people. Dedeaux's team was ranked No. 1 in the country, but the NCAA

Tom Kelly, left, and Danuska Kelly celebrate with Rod Dedeaux. *Photo courtesy of Tom Kelly*

decided it was not eligible to go back to Omaha for the College World Series. After the tournament was over, USC's team was still listed No. 1 on every publication, so Dedeaux went out and bought rings for every member. I'm sure he died still wearing his.

Dedeaux always spoke about two games. One was the 1948 College World Series playoff game, in which USC beat Yale 9-2 to win the title. Future president George H.W. Bush, a left-handed-hitting first baseman, was left waiting in the on-deck circle.

The other game was also played back in Omaha in 1973. It was the third of five consecutive national titles—a feat that will never be duplicated. To get to the title game against Arizona State, USC had to beat Minnesota, which was led by Dave Winfield, who could have played in the NFL or NBA had he not become a Major League Baseball Hall of Fame outfielder. Minnesota had USC down 9-0, but the Trojans rallied to beat Winfield, an outstanding pitcher, 10-9. Winfield was still named the series MVP. When I saw Dave recently, I told him that Dedeaux loved to recall that game.

I was standing in front of the dugout one time at Dedeaux Field when I noticed the coach was talking to a young man whose name I never knew. He was giving him that dry wash, his hand in the middle of his back.

"Now listen, Tiger . . . ," I heard him tell the player, and on he went. By the time Dedeaux finished and I was ready to interview him, the kid had a smile as big as daybreak and ran onto the field with his glove.

"Is he your starting pitcher? Starting outfielder?" I asked Dedeaux.

"Oh, he won't play today," Dedeaux said. "I won't need him."

"But all that talk you just gave him . . ."

Dedeaux said, "Listen to me. That Tiger, if I call upon him, will be ready. And he'll be ready because I've got that Tiger ready to play."

That was his philosophy. And everybody was named "Tiger." Dedeaux would spend minutes, even hours, to make sure you knew that no matter where you were on the bench, you were ready to play.

There's a member I see regularly at Riviera Country Club named Skip Taft. Before he became a very successful lawyer, he was a left-handed pitcher for Dedeaux. He told me that Dedeaux used to come up to him and say, "Now listen, Skip, I want you to give me a little BP and then keep yourself ready because I may need you in the sixth or seventh inning." To this day, Skip will smile and tell me the fact that Dedeaux wanted him to play for him was one of the greatest feelings in the world. Skip was never a big-time performer, but he was a Dedeaux man.

I was the master of ceremonies for the coach's 90th birthday celebration at Dedeaux Field. You talk about the sharpest knife in the drawer—that was Dedeaux. As many as 70 players came from all over the country, including Japan, to honor him. Some were famous in baseball, but some had gone on to great success in other endeavors. They'd walk up to him and ask how he was doing, etc.

I wanted to know what was going on, so I'd ask Dedeaux, "Who was that?"

He'd say, "That's so-and-so. Batted .264, had 12 homers, drove in 40. Great glove, not a great hitter . . . "

He knew every one of them. When they heard him recite their careers, chapter and verse, they looked as though they had never had a happier moment.

The head coach was truly blessed. In 47 years at the university, I can't think of anybody who ever received a better response than Rod Dedeaux. Who else could get Mickey Mantle to come out to USC for a home-run hitting contest in the off-season? He also had great ties with the Dodgers, playing an exhibition series against the team each March. I don't know if the Dodgers ever played a college team again.

Dedeaux had season seats in the loge level at the end of the press box between third and home at Dodger Stadium. I sat up there with him from time to time. And he was every bit as big an icon at Dodger Stadium, walking in with a cane that was actually a baseball bat covered in signatures.

People had such great respect for Dedeaux. I'm not sure anyone else but the Cardinal would have allowed Dr. Arthur Bartner to bring the USC band to Dedeaux's memorial service at Our Lady of Angels Church in downtown L.A. I also attended another service, where I got to speak. I told the people that we were honoring a man whose grandchildren stand up in front of an entire congregation and tell everyone how much they love him. I spoke about what a success he was in business, his avocation coaching USC baseball, and what a truly warm, fulfilling life he had. I said, "And every man I know, including myself, would say, 'He didn't deserve that. There had to be something that went wrong.' All of his children loved him. They went to USC; their children went to USC. He lived a long life with a lovely woman. I don't know anyone who ever had a bad thing to say about him. It's unreal. It's unnatural. For us mortal humans, it seemed unfair."

I kidded Tommy Lasorda, who was in Hawaii during the ceremony and sent his eulogy on tape for everyone to see. Lasorda talked about how close he and Dedeaux were, and how, one night, they'd been out doing the Lord's work when they became hungry around 11:30. Everywhere they wanted to eat was closed. Lasorda said he'd call his wife, Jo, and tell her that he and Rod were coming home for dinner at midnight. Lasorda talked about it as if it was a gourmet meal: they had spaghetti and meatballs and a salad with Italian dressing. That was the gourmet meal Lasorda had been bragging about? For an Irishman like me, a gourmet meal is a six-pack of beer and a boiled potato.

Dedeaux was one of the prime movers of Olympic baseball and he was proud of it. When we had him in the booth, he'd talk about the dream that was finally realized at Dedeaux Field, which I call Cooperstown West. Now there's a shrine to show all that he and his family put together. When you think of all the great players and their achievements under Dedeaux—from Tom Seaver, Dave Kingman, Fred Lynn, Roy Smalley, and Don Buford to Mark McGwire and Randy Johnson—I don't think his success will be duplicated anywhere. In fact, at the most recent gathering of the Trojans' Hall of Fame banquet, Dedeaux nearly received a standing ovation when his face appeared on the screen of recently departed Hall of Famers.

FORREST TWOGOOD (1907-1972)
USC HEAD BASKETBALL COACH: 1951-1966
- 252 WINS, 178 LOSSES
- LOST TO BRADLEY IN NCAA NATIONAL SEMIFINAL (1954)
- LOST TO UTAH IN DISTRICT 8 PLAYOFF GAME (1960)
- MADE FAR WEST REGIONAL FINAL, LOST TO ARIZONA STATE AND LOYOLA (1961)

THE FORREST TWOGOOD MEMORIAL AWARD IS GIVEN ANNUALLY TO USC'S BEST DEFENSIVE PLAYER

Having been elected into the Illinois Sports Broadcasting Hall of Fame and having broadcast the Illinois high school championships for 28 years, I always thought I knew something about basketball.

When I came to USC in 1961, the first team I saw was Forrest Twogood's Trojans, with Ken Stanley, Chris Appel, Gordie Martin, Pete Hillman, and center John Rudometkin. I wasn't really that impressed. Rudometkin, who entered into the USC Hall of Fame the same year I did, looked like a guy who had his foot caught in a revolving door. But every time he turned and flew, arms akimbo, the ball somehow went into the net.

In those days, despite the fact that USC's history included Bill Sharman, Alex Hanum, and Tex Winter, I don't think basketball was that big of an item—certainly not as big as it was in the Midwest.

But Forrest Twogood, who only had three losing seasons in 16 years at USC, and I had a great relationship. It was just a delight hearing about the days he spent pitching with Dizzy Dean in the St. Louis Cardinals organization in the '30s. John McKay even used him as a football scout.

Twogood was a great all-around coach, and let it be known that he brought the first black basketball player to the university. Verne Ashby, who actually went to the school on an academic scholarship, came to USC out of Manual Arts High.

BOB BOYD
USC BASKETBALL PLAYER: 1950-1952
USC HEAD BASKETBALL COACH: 1967-1979
    216 WINS, 131 LOSSES
    WON 24 GAMES WITH 1971 AND 1974 TEAMS
    MADE FOUR POSTSEASON TOURNAMENTS (1979 NCAA, 1973 NIT, 1974 AND 1975 COMMISSIONER'S CONFERENCE)
    WINS OVER UCLA IN 1969 (46-44) AND 1970 (87-86) WERE THE BRUINS' FIRST LOSSES IN PAULEY PAVILION (BETWEEN 1965, WHEN THE PAVILION WAS BUILT, AND 1975, THE BRUINS HAD A 149-2 RECORD)
    2-26 VS. UCLA
USC ATHLETIC HALL OF FAME: 1997

Tom Kelly, second from left, poses with USC head basketball coach Forrest Twogood, second from right, along with assistants Tony Psaltis, right, and Billy Mulligan, left.
Photo courtesy of Tom Kelly

It's easy to write Bob Boyd off as someone who happened to be on the wrong end of a coaching battle against UCLA's John Wooden. But Boyd faced many of the same problems at USC that his predecessor, Forrest Twogood, did.

Twogie and I were once in Wyoming, where the team was playing against the Cowboys. Everett Case, a longtime successful coach at North Carolina State in the '40s, '50s, and '60s, happened to be at this game, and he and I spoke of the fact that a coach's legacy is related to how many trophies he has in the trophy case. We also talked about the program irregularity and point-shaving accusations that appeared after the coach won some of his own titles with the Wolfpack. People said that these titles were tainted. Case said that no one is ever going to know whether any of it was true. When he looked in the record books, the titles were there—they'd go on forever and couldn't be taken away.

A number of great coaches have come within a whistle of winning everything. Jim Valvano had just one title at North Carolina State and Al McGuire had just one title at Marquette. Each of those championships represents the one great moment each coach had in an illustrious career.

An MVP on one of Twogood's teams, Boyd could have fallen into that category. But, due in large part to rules that restricted conference champions to the NCAA tournament only, it didn't happen.

I think Billy Mulligan, who later coached at UC Irvine, could have been the man to replace Twogood. Mulligan was a great assistant at USC, but one of his family members was autistic, and those issues came first. But Boyd played some great games against Wooden. Boyd also had some magnificent talented players, from Paul Westphal to Gus Johnson and Mo Layton to Ron Riley. Jim Hefner, Boyd's alter ego, was also a great recruiter for the team. Hefner got Westphal to come to USC at a time when the university was still selling the fact that they planned to build a new arena for the program—something that wasn't complete until recently, when Galen Center was built.

We all know the rule of thumb that success breeds success. Although his father had been a team captain at USC, Gail Goodrich joined Wooden. Once he went to UCLA, the school was recruiting players like Jack Hirsh, Fred Slaughter, and Walt Hazzard. While UCLA won the championship in '64, Boyd didn't have that kind of success to draw on. Even today, players want to go where the winners are. But Boyd was never one to say, "Coulda, shoulda, woulda." He played the cards dealt to him and became a much better coach than many give him credit for.

No question about it, he may never get his due. That's what happens to guys who finish second. Boyd wasn't appreciated because a man right down the freeway received all the headlines. I can only imagine what

OTHER USC NOTABLES

Tommy Prothro, Pepper Rogers, and, to some extent, Terry Donahue had to go through when John McKay and John Robinson were constantly winning on the football field. They, like Boyd, deserve more recognition.

Boyd and Bob Knight were great friends, and Boyd liked to run Knight's motion offense. I remember one game back in 1974, when USC and Indiana met at the Kiel Arena in St. Louis for what they called the Commissioner's Tournament. All conference winners went to the NCAA Tournament, while the National Invitation Tournament, which had been around since the late '30s, would try to get other great teams to play. Hoping to destroy the NIT, the Commissioner's Tournament took all second-place teams for an event of its own.

Boyd and Knight were talking to one another before the game when I came down with my tape recorder. I sat with them, waiting to interview Boyd. Eventually, Knight turned to me and said, "What the — are you doing here? Can't you see we're talking? Get out of here."

Boyd finally stepped in and told him, "Hey, he's my announcer; he's here to tape a pregame interview."

Knight was as ornery as he could be.

Indiana won the game, and Knight reluctantly came out to get the trophy. He then announced that he didn't even want to go to the "damn tournament," gave the trophy to Indiana's president, and walked away.

Years later, I was waiting to hit on a par-three hole in a golf tournament in Vail, Colorado, when Bob Knight appeared. I hadn't seen him in years. He walked right over, shook my hand, and asked how I was doing. I was just amazed he knew my name.

In 1977, Pete Newell and I did games for Prime Ticket. We were having breakfast with Boyd and Dick Perry, the USC athletic director, before a game in Austin, Texas. The Trojans had just lost to Dale Brown and Louisiana State 87-76 out in Baton Rouge.

Out of the clear blue, Boyd said to Perry, "I want a new contract."

Perry almost choked on his hash browns.

"I want a new contract or I'm leaving," Boyd repeated.

Perry finally responded, "I'm trying to save your job. You're 14-12."

When he and Perry finished their discussion, I asked Boyd, "Do you have another job to go to?'

He said, "No, why?"

"Well, I'm kind of stupid myself to have worked in this town all these years without an agent, but I do know you don't tell the guy you're leaving one job until you have another offer on the table."

They lost the game to Texas 66-61. Boyd, who didn't receive a new contract, left USC two years later, sat out a season, and then turned up at Mississippi State, which played its games in a city named Starkville. This may give you a clue as to the atmosphere there.

A few years later, Boyd became the athletic director at Chapman College. While we were playing golf together one day, he told me about this fundraiser he was going to have. He was going to ask Tom Selleck to be his featured speaker.

It sounded like a great idea, considering Selleck was this handsome actor known as *Magnum, P.I.* Two months later, though, Boyd said that Selleck never answered his letter.

"Has the thought occurred to you," I asked Boyd, "that had you played him maybe two or three minutes a game he may have been more willing to help you out?"

Selleck was a Detroit native who'd always dreamed of attending USC. He walked on to Boyd's team and eventually earned a tuition-only scholarship, but, as Selleck would later say, his only claim to fame on the Trojans' squad was playing the role of Lew Alcindor in practice to prepare the team for UCLA.

"You know, that thought did occur to me," Boyd said. But it was apparently too late.

Years later, at Rod Dedeaux's funeral, I saw Selleck and his brother, Bill. When I mentioned the story to him, Selleck said he didn't think he ever received that letter.

OTHER USC NOTABLES

I really enjoy the fact that current USC basketball coach Tim Floyd has included Boyd in recent uniform retirement celebrations. When Paul Westphal's number was retired, the former coach stood up to introduce the Trojan of the past. Boyd coached through some tough times, but he did a great job for the university. I'm glad he's still remembered.

STAN MORRISON
USC HEAD BASKETBALL COACH: 1980-1986
103 WINS, 95 LOSSES

Stan Morrison was so brilliant that, at age 20, he may have been the youngest architect ever to come out of the University of California. He recruited three of the best players who never had a chance to play at USC—Bo Kimble, Hank Gathers, and Tommy Lewis. After some sort of recruiting miscue, Kimble and Gathers left to Loyola Marymount and Lewis went to Pepperdine. Gathers' life ended tragically, while Kimble went on to play briefly in the NBA. Not that long ago, I saw Lewis, who is now the coach at JSerra Catholic High in Orange County, California. He still looks as if he could play today.

GEORGE RAVELING
USC HEAD BASKETBALL COACH: 1987-1994
115 WINS, 118 LOSSES

While coaching at USC, George Raveling's greatest coup was landing Harold Minor, otherwise known as "Baby Jordan," out of Inglewood High. Minor was one of the most soft-spoken, nicest human beings and became one of the all-time greats in Trojans history. What an unbelievable shooter—the best I've ever seen in my life.

While I was working at KNX, this big UCLA fan would call me three times a week, claiming, "Baby Jordan is going to Westwood." I'd always pretend I did not know who he was talking about, but, to my knowledge, Minor was all but going to be a Bruin—until he ended up with the Trojans.

Minor's name came up in a conversation at Michael Jordan's adult basketball camp in Las Vegas a few years ago, and I finally asked George, "How did you ever get him to come to USC?"

"First, he was never going to UCLA; he was going to Notre Dame," George replied. "So I went to visit Harold, his mother, and his mother's sister in Inglewood. And it turned out the one who really decided it all was Harold's aunt. That's how he ended up at USC."

I have a great affection for George. A dear friend and first-class human being, he probably reads seven newspapers every day from all over the country and is conversant on anything from the government to the price of tea in China. Though he now travels the world as a representative for Nike, the great success he met at so many different places proved that he could coach anywhere he went.

One of my favorite Raveling quotes came when George was coaching at Washington State, in Pullman, Washington. Someone once asked him if it was the end of the world.

"No, but you can see it from there," he'd say.

Toward the end of George's career at USC, he had some real success, splitting some season series with UCLA as the powerhouse headed toward March Madness. Charlie Parker, who I used to call "Yardbird" after the great jazz saxophonist, replaced him.

It was truly sad that George had to leave coaching at USC in 1994 at the age of only 57. He spent 55 days in a hospital recuperating from a car accident in which he was blindsided. He broke his pelvis, nine ribs, and his collarbone and suffered a collapsed lung and traumatized heart. George said he had no more energy to coach after the doctor told him that had he been let out of the hospital any earlier, he probably would have gone home to die. In March of '95, George helped CBS do its NCAA Tournament broadcast, and eventually, he worked with me on USC basketball games.

OTHER USC NOTABLES

HENRY BIBBY
USC HEAD BASKETBALL COACH: 1997-2005
  131 WINS, 111 LOSSES
  THREE NCAA TOURNAMENT APPEARANCES (1997, 2001, 2002)
  ELITE EIGHT (2001)

Henry Bibby was unusual, to say the least. He came from a great athletic family; his brother, Jim, was an exceptional major-league pitcher. Henry was on UCLA's NCAA title team in 1972, and, as an NBA rookie, the New York Knicks' title team in '73. But once his playing days ended, he seemed to toil in anonymity. Bibby may have developed an attitude in which he looked at everyone with a jaundice eye as he searched for any coaching position. He was a strict disciplinarian whose players had to do what they were told.

I think one of the biggest compliments he paid me was given when I interviewed him on the *Trojan Magazine* TV show. We talked about games played and games coming up. After he had appeared on the show three weeks in a row, he got up out of his chair and said, "You can come to my practice any time you want and you don't even have to call." An individual from the sports information department said they'd never seen Bibby make that kind of offer before, so I thought we had a pretty good rapport.

I enjoyed his teams. They were tough and competitive. Though he may have regretted that his skills as a player or coach weren't recognized by many people in the basketball business, Bibby recruited good kids and even took them to the field of eight one year.

People made a big fuss over the fact that USC had hired a former UCLA great to be its coach, but I don't think Bibby had an allegiance to anyone. Estranged from his son, Mike, he had to have endured a great deal. He may have been a tough father. A lot of us have been and live to regret it. After getting to know him, I'd ask him about Mike and he would smile proudly, but I don't think they conversed much. It's unfortunate, but it happens more often than people realize.

TIM FLOYD
USC HEAD BASKETBALL COACH: 2005-PRESENT
42 WINS, 25 LOSSES
SWEET 16 FINISH IN 2007 NCAA TOURNAMENT (DEFEATING ARKANSAS AND TEXAS BEFORE LOSING TO NO. 1 SEED NORTH CAROLINA)

The last time USC's basketball program made it as far as the Elite Eight in the Big Dance, Henry Bibby was coaching them, but in 2007, Tim Floyd was very near that field of eight when his team lost to North Carolina. What a magnificent coaching job Floyd did! For those critics who say that football is USC's game and basketball belongs to the guys cross-town, don't be a bit surprised if, with the advent of Galen Center, a magnificent arena, and the expert coaching and recruiting that Floyd has exhibited, USC becomes a power to be recognized on the court as well. I wish him the best.

WOLFE, TOLEY, LEACH, DALAND . . .

When you talk about USC coaches, bear in mind that football, basketball, and baseball aren't the only sports in which they can win. I may have broadcast only a couple events a year in track and field, tennis, and swimming, but I knew who the stars were. And I had to know the coaches who made the programs work.

You can't overlook the accomplishments of Vern Wolfe (USC track and field coach, 1963-1984), who began as a pole vaulter at USC in the late '40s and went on to coach six athletes—Dallas Long, Rex Crawley, Mike Larrabee, Bob Seagren, Randy Williams, and Don Quarrie—who later won Olympic track and field goal medals. His teams finished 106-17-1 in dual meets.

In the years O.J. Simpson ran on the football field, Wolfe won three NCAA titles, two outdoors and an indoor. He also put together the famous record-setting 4x100 team.

OTHER USC NOTABLES

Following Wolfe, after both Ed Bullard and Jim Bush, was Ron Allice. He brings such great enthusiasm to the program. Allice, whose protégés include Dwight Stones, is so dedicated to what he's doing and to the players he coaches. Plus, he has a new track and field stadium.

George Toley (USC tennis coach, 1954-1980) had a career mark of 430-92-4 with 10 NCAA titles. He had a great connection in landing Mexican national talent, including Raul Ramirez. Every now and then, usually when USC was playing UCLA, I was able to broadcast a match. One year, USC, who had both Stan Smith and Bob Lutz, played against a great UCLA team led by Ian Crookendon. This was back before tiebreakers; you had to win by two. The final match went 19-17 before Crookendon beat Smith. I thought whoever had to edit the broadcast into an hour show would have to work for a week.

Toley had a fantastic career, and was followed by Dick Leach (USC tennis coach, 1980-2002), who had just as great a run. After closing his career with the last of four NCAA title teams, Leach had tears coming down his cheeks as we did the Trojan Sports Report for Fox on campus. He told me how his 11th seeded team had managed to beat the Bulldogs in Athens, Georgia, and had dedicated their appearance to him.

As for swimming, it seems as if the only great athlete Peter Daland (USC swimming coach, 1957-1992) was unable to deliver to USC was Mark Spitz. USC had nine national titles under Daland.

And we can't forget what Mike Gillespie (USC baseball coach, 1987-2006) did once he took over for Rod Dedeaux. Gillespie, who played on one of Dedeaux's championship teams, coached one himself 14 years later. When you consider the scholarship limitations a baseball coach now has to deal with, on top of the fact that major-league scouts already know who the top players are and lure them into professional leagues for bigger money, Gillespie was very successful.

In golf, one guy I think should be in the USC Athletic Hall of Fame is Stan Wood (USC golf coach, 1955-1979). Take a look at all the great golfers who've come to USC. The list—Sam Randolph, Al Geiberger, Foster Bradley, Craig Stadler, and Dave Stockton—contains a Masters champion, a U.S. Amateur winner, and a couple of PGA champions. Wood recruited them all, but he's never really received his just due.

And let's not forget the ladies. The Linda Sharp (USC women's basketball coach, 1977-1989) teams of 1982 and '83 were led by Cheryl Miller and the McGee twins. Many thought Cheryl would be a better shooter than her brother, Reggie, in a game of horse. And a couple players were akin to her. Lisa Leslie is one of the greatest athletes ever to go to any university. I don't think anyone in her sport has won the international acclaim that she has. She's a delightful woman. I used to kid her that she was just too tall for me, or else we'd have made a very romantic couple. She'd just look down at me and laugh. She is very interested in the lives of African-American women and has held classes back in Inglewood to help them pursue their dreams.

5

THE NOTRE DAME MYSTIQUE IS NO MISTAKE

THE FIRST FOOTBALL GAME I EVER SAW was at South Bend, Indiana. I was five years old, and my dad, my uncle, and my cousin—who later played at Notre Dame—drove from Minneapolis to South Bend to see the Irish play Minnesota. I had no recollection of the game, just that it was a big outing. Two of my cousins actually attended the university, and I always felt like a subway alum, as most Irish Catholics would through the years.

It was Knute Rockne's wife who convinced him that the Irish, who were then known as the Ramblers, should leave South Bend every other season to play the Trojans. The kids would enjoy it and they'd be in better weather. Everything fell into place for a series that prospered every season with the exception of the war years of '43 and '44. What a magnificent relationship.

No matter what team records are—though fortunately, both universities have been highly regarded and very competitive—the game is truly an illustrious event. USC-UCLA is a great fight. So is Texas-Oklahoma, Alabama-Auburn, Minnesota-Wisconsin, and Michigan-Ohio State. But USC and Notre Dame are a national pair. No matter how good or indifferent Notre Dame's season has been, when you consider its subway alumni, the game rises to national prominence. It's unbelievable. Notre Dame seems to be the keystone in college football because of its national following.

HARD TIMES

I remember my first visit back to Notre Dame as a broadcaster. Notre Dame had a far better team than USC that year. The team suffered a 30-0 loss on a terrible day in the middle of October. It tried to snow, but just turned to rain.

The stadium had a big strip, maybe 15 to 20 feet, of solid concrete that stretched from the end of the field to the first row of seats. Bill Nelsen was the USC quarterback. I can still see Nelsen getting hit, being driven out of bounds, and rolling around on that concrete like a rubber toy.

A VISITATION

I was very familiar with all the legendary figures of Notre Dame. Near the end of an undefeated season under John McKay in 1962, USC was preparing for another big game at the Coliseum against Notre Dame. Someone said that famous former coach Frank Leahy was in the press box. I thought they were kidding, though I knew he was going to San Diego as the general manager of the NFL's Chargers, who were about to leave L.A.

I ran around the press box until I found Leahy. I then introduced myself and told him I'd love to have him on the show at halftime. And Leahy, who could just charm the birds out of the trees, said, "Son, it would be a delight."

Two minutes before the end of the first half, the door to our booth opened and Leahy walked in. Everyone in the booth was just agog. The

---

Tom Kelly makes his way down the Coliseum seats toward the field during a USC game in the 1960s. *Photo courtesy of Tom Kelly*

score at halftime was 18-0, USC. Darryl Lamonica, the former Bakersfield star, was the Irish quarterback. Although he had a great career at Notre Dame, he was not having a good game.

I talked to Leahy about the great Irish program, his future plans, and his history. He was unbelievable.

Near the end of halftime, USC came out of the tunnel, followed by Notre Dame. I asked Leahy, "Coach, what's gonna happen in the second half?"

He put his arm around me and, as I heard the Irish fight song playing down below, he said, "Tom, as the sun sinks over the rim of this mighty Coliseum, the sons of Notre Dame will come marching up the field to victory. Thank you, God bless, and good afternoon." And he just drifted out of the booth.

I'm thinking, "My God, I just got a visitation." I couldn't even cue the commercial.

It was amazing.

Fortunately, USC won the game 25-0, and the Irish did not come marching up the field.

USHERED IN

Years later, in 1971, USC went to South Bend to play Notre Dame. I took my oldest son, Kevin, who was only 13 years old but already 6-foot-4. It was raining as we drove into the lot, so I pointed out the press box elevator and told Kevin to wait for me there while I parked the car. I made it to the press box elevator just in time for the press box attendant to say, "Nope, you can't go up there."

I asked, "What's going on?"

The guy said, "He's too young to go into the press box."

I said, "He's not going into the press box. He's going with me into one of those terrible little three feet by four feet sheds you've built up there on the roof, and I'm broadcasting the game from there."

"Nope, you can't."

"Well, then, I think we have a real problem, because I'm going to do this game and he's going with me."

We continued to argue back and forth when the door to that tiny elevator suddenly opened. Out stepped Frank Leahy with a couple of Indiana state troopers. I had not seen him since 1962, but for whatever reason, he walked out, put his arm around me, and said, "Tom, how are you?"

The usher looked at me. Then Leahy said, "Who's this fine looking lad here?"

"My son, Kevin."

So he talked to my son a while and then asked, "You're doing the game?"

"Yes, I am."

"Boy, I'd like to stay for it, but I'm not feeling well and I've got to go," he said. "God bless; have a great game." And with that, he and his escorts got in the state trooper car and drove away. Leahy would end up passing away a couple years later from leukemia.

After that exchange, the usher said to me, "Right this way."

I replied, "Well, aren't you a big guy? Let me tell you something. There are two pictures hanging in that building over there. One is Frank Leahy and the other is Knute Rockne. And now you're going to walk me through that crummy press box so I can go on the roof? What a sport you are."

I've thought about the exchange a million times since then. It's easy to wonder now what would have happened had I continued to argue with the usher and finally climbed through the stands to do that game. Hmm.

DIRECTING THE ATHLETIC DIRECTOR

Once, Craig Fertig and I did the broadcast for Prime Ticket at South Bend. At that time, Father Joyce was the president of Notre Dame and Dick Rosenthal was the athletic director. Fertig and I were standing on the rooftop, doing our opening. Behind us was Touchdown Jesus. Rosenthal and Joyce were up there watching us tape everything. When we finished, they both applauded.

Being the nasty guy I am to begin with, I said, "What did you guys expect, a shank or something?" They had a good laugh.

"Say, since I've got you here, Rosenthal," I continued, "let me ask you a question while I'm here on the roof of this lousy tin shack you call a press box. You've got all the money in the world and a ton of land off that major freeway that runs from Chicago to Pennsylvania. Why don't you build a stadium out there for 80,000? NBC would give you all the money you'd need. Just put ramps on both sides of the interstate. This is a great place, but even you know that after the game, you spend two hours stuck in traffic just to get back to that freeway. It's terrible."

Rosenthal looked at me and said, "You know, I was asleep the other night when I suddenly woke up at two in the morning and Rockne was standing right there at the end of my bed."

Joyce stared at him in confusion.

Rosenthal continued, "Rockne said, 'What is this stuff I hear about rebuilding the stadium and moving it?' I couldn't say anything to him. Rockne then went on: 'Let me tell you something. Don't ever think of messing with Notre Dame football.' Then Rockne disappeared."

Rosenthal paused and said, "Now, if you think I want Rockne to haunt me the rest of my life, you're crazy. We're staying here."

And, with that, Joyce turned and walked away.

McKAY'S DELAY

Before another game at Notre Dame, John McKay, who was by then the coach at Tampa Bay, went to the USC dressing room to give the team a pep talk. Afterward, he said he was going to come up to the press box and go on the air with me.

The first quarter went by. No McKay.

Halfway into the second quarter, he came up to the box and slammed the door shut. He was just livid. I asked him what had happened.

"I talked to the team. Incidentally, the opening kickoff was fumbled and returned by Notre Dame for a touchdown 15 seconds into the game," said McKay. "I left the dressing room and had to use the restroom."

McKay had to go down a series of steps deep into Notre Dame Stadium. While he was in the restroom, a janitor came by and locked the door. Over 60,000 people were screaming and raising 14 different kinds of hell after that opening kickoff as McKay was hammering on the door, trying to get out. After the first quarter settled down and the game turned into a Notre Dame rout, the noise quieted and the guy with the broom heard McKay's pounding, opened the door, and let him out.

A BROADCASTER AND A PRIEST

I invited Ray George, a former USC offensive lineman from the '30s and a coach for McKay, up to the booth during a trip to Notre Dame. When I finally made it up to the press box, I found our game engineer jammed into a corner. Ray was standing there, along with a priest. I put things down and, after about 10 minutes, turned to Ray and asked, "Aren't you going to introduce me to your friend, the priest?"

Ray said, "I thought he was your friend . . . "

"So who are you?" I asked.

He said, "I'm a secular priest from Terre Haute. They invited me up for the game, but they didn't have a seat for me. So they said I could go up here and watch from one of these booths."

After sizing up the situation, I finally said, "Let me tell you something, Father. You see that big fella? He's a Trojan through and through. If either one of us sees you even remotely praying for Notre Dame, I'll have him throw you right out of this booth."

"Oh heavens no," he replied.

And he remained very quiet in the booth with us throughout another Irish win.

ONCE IRISH, ALWAYS IRISH

They say once a Trojan, always a Trojan. But John Huarte, the 1964 Heisman Trophy winner out of Mater Dei High, showed me that the same goes for the Irish.

We had the same dentist, Dr. Bill Francis, in Pacific Palisades. While at the office for a visit, Dr. Francis said, "Know who's here? John Huarte."

"Oh, great! I'd love to say hello to him."

Huarte was half asleep when Dr. Francis walked over and opened his mouth.

"Take a look at that," he said.

A molar in the back, left side of his mouth was encrusted in gold. In green, the words "Go Irish" were inscribed.

I couldn't believe it.

A DISTANT MEMORY

Ed "Moose" Krause, a former player of Rockne's and the school's athletic director, was another frequent visitor to the press box at halftime. We interviewed him almost every year, regardless of whether the game was in Los Angeles or South Bend, and it finally dawned on me that he couldn't remember my name.

So I waited until he was in the booth with us once before I told the audience the score and said, on air, "It's halftime here, and I'm Tom Kelly. Ed 'Moose' Krause, the athletic director at Notre Dame, joins us in a moment." I came back from a commercial and repeated the exact same thing. Then I said, "Ed, good to have you on the air again."

And he replied, "Thank you, Jim."

Now, he did that to me all the time, almost to the point that I had decided to wear a nametag.

I once told this story to Huarte and Jack Snow, the latter of whom was an Irish star receiver out of Long Beach in the early '60s.

Snow said, "Let me tell you, all the years we were there at Notre Dame, when we'd walk across the campus, we'd often run into Moose Krause. And he'd give John a big hug and say, 'Boy that was a great game you played last Saturday.' And he'd look at me and say, 'You had a great game too, but I can't remember your name.' It wasn't until I graduated that he finally figured my name out, so don't feel so bad."

I only saw Krause once a year for 15 years and he never got it right, but I eventually took it in stride.

6

A DOZEN GAMES, PLAYS, AND PLAYERS FOR THE AGES

PEOPLE ASK ME ALL THE TIME about the favorite football games I've covered. My gosh. I've been privy to many of the greatest ever played. I think there was a book that recently came out listing the top 10 games in USC history, and either I was at or saw seven of them.

Great games elicit memories of great players, and vice versa. They've gone hand in hand throughout the years. I honestly can't do the games justice by ranking them in any order, but I'll start with 12, and you decide which one ends up as No. 1 on your list.

JANUARY 1, 1963, ROSE BOWL
(NO. 1) USC 42, (NO. 2) WISCONSIN 37

	1ST	2ND	3RD	4TH	FINAL
WISCONSIN	7	0	7	23	37
USC	7	14	14	7	42

Quick Summary: USC quarterback Pete Beathard had put his team ahead 35-14 after three quarters with one touchdown pass to Ron Butcher (15 yards) and two to Hal Bedsole (57 and 23 yards). Fullback Ben Wilson (1 yard) and halfback Ron Heller (25 yards) also ran the ball in for touchdowns. Beathard tossed a 13-yard TD pass to Fred Hill for a 28-point lead, but that's when Wisconsin fifth-year senior quarterback Ron VanderKelen led a comeback, hitting receiver Pat Richter on a 19-yard touchdown with 1:19 remaining to *close the gap to five. Willie Brown, USC's star two-way player with 108 yards receiving, intercepted a VanderKelen pass in the end zone to prevent a touchdown during the Badgers' comeback. VanderKelen completed 33 of 48 passes for 401 yards, with Richter catching 11 for 163 yards. Beathard was named MVP of the game.*

If this wasn't the best, it wasn't bad for the Voice of the Trojans, who was in the Rose Bowl for the first time.

I had worked all season with my new broadcast partner, Bill Symes, who had done games at Stanford at the time of the "Vow Boys" in the mid-'30s and with Frankie Albert in the early '40s before he joined his family's Cadillac dealership. KNX sports director Pat McGuirck, a Stanford grad himself, knew Symes well.

But NBC paired me with Mike Walden, who had been doing the University of Wisconsin games, to broadcast this contest on national radio. I would do the first half, and Mike, who broadcast many USC and UCLA events after moving to Southern California, would do the second half.

Tom Gallery was the game producer, and Mike and I met him at the Sheraton Hotel beforehand. Gallery said, "Neither of you has any relatives that you want to wish a happy new year on the telecast, is that clear? If I hear one word of that, this broadcast is off the air." It scared the devil out of both of us.

The lighting at the Rose Bowl was terrible. The game started late, after 2 p.m., and as the afternoon wore on, the sky grew darker and darker. USC was wearing the Cardinal uniforms. As a result, Ron VanderKelen and his Badgers teammates were wearing white uniforms—that's all you could make out by the end. It was as if they were playing a shadow game.

USC coach John McKay, whose team led 42-14 going into the final quarter, made a great comment about this matchup: "I thought the rest of the coaches could handle it from that point on. I was in the car going home down the freeway." He wasn't, of course, but he could have been.

A DOZEN GAMES, PLAYS, AND PLAYERS FOR THE AGES

Just for the excitement, it was one of the most memorable Rose Bowl games for years.

NOVEMBER 28, 1964
USC 20, (NO. 1) NOTRE DAME 17

	1ST	2ND	3RD	4TH	FINAL
NOTRE DAME	3	14	0	0	17
USC	0	0	7	13	20

Quick Summary: USC, a 12-point underdog in its final game of the season, trailed 17-0 at the half before 83,840 fans at the Coliseum. A Mike Garrett 1-yard touchdown put the Trojans on the board in the third quarter. In the final quarter, senior quarterback Craig Fertig hit Fred Hill with a 21-yard scoring pass. Then, with 1:33 remaining, a 15-yard Fertig touchdown pass to Rod Sherman completed the upset and gave the Irish their only loss of the season. Garrett had 79 yards on 21 carries and four receptions for 28 yards, while Fertig completed 15 of 23 passes—seven of which were caught by Sherman for 109 yards—for 225 yards. Irish senior quarterback John Huarte, who would go on to win the Heisman Trophy, completed 18 of 29 passes for 272 yards, including a 21-yard touchdown toss to Jack Snow in the second quarter. The Trojans believed that if they won the game, they would be voted into the Rose Bowl, but the Athletic Association of Western Universities sent Oregon State to Pasadena. The Beavers lost to Michigan 34-7 in the 1965 Rose Bowl. What was the highlight moment for Oregon State? Kicking on third down.

The back of USC's 1964 highlight album said, "The 1964 finale . . . [was] the greatest Trojans thriller of all time, eclipsing even the memorable 16-14 shocker at South Bend in 1931. Not even the most

---

After the 1963 Rose Bowl Victory over Wisconsin, the national championship trophy is presented to USC president Dr. Norman Topping, second from left, while Tom Kelly, second from right, and USC player Ben Wilson, far right, look on before the Tommy Trojan statue on campus. *Photo courtesy of Tom Kelly*

talented Hollywood script writer could have come up with one to match this '64 clincher. If somebody brave or foolish enough to suggest such an ending had offered it for free, he would have been laughed out of the court. But it actually happened . . . to unbeaten Notre Dame's dismay and to the delight of USC followers as McKay's miracle men made a mockery of the impossible . . . "

I must tell you that my critics through the years—not necessarily Trojans fans, but those who may have liked USC and were skeptical about my broadcasting the games—seem to remember that, when Craig Fertig threw his final pass and Rod Sherman caught it, this unbiased announcer shouted, "We win!" Actually, I did say that, but not until the game was over, because John Huarte and Jack Snow were still throwing and catching passes right down to the final play.

A dear friend of mine who was giving away his daughter at her wedding service in Santa Barbara told me that he was screaming right along with everyone else at the church when he heard me make that touchdown call.

Although it was one of those games in which USC was inside the 20-yard line four or five times and couldn't score and Notre Dame led 17-0 at the half, something stopped the Irish. John McKay gave one of his famous halftime speeches that day. It went, "Gentlemen, we are down 17 to 0. If we don't score at least 17 points in the second half, we are going to lose this football game."

Now, Notre Dame was knocking at the door again in the third quarter when Nick Buoniconti, the great Irish two-way player at offensive line and linebacker, was called for a penalty. From third-and-short it became third-and-15. The Irish didn't get the first down, and USC took over. Fertig hit Fred Hill in the near corner, but it was ruled out of bounds. On the next play, Fertig got rid of the ball as the great Alan Page came up to tackle him. Fertig's pass was ruled incomplete, but he wasn't called for a fumble. On fourth down, Page hit Fertig again on a blitz. The ball sailed through the air, Sherman caught it, and USC won. Fertig never saw the completion. And if you go back and

A DOZEN GAMES, PLAYS, AND PLAYERS FOR THE AGES

watch a tape of the game, you can see a guy standing next to the scoreboard clock at the Coliseum, jumping up and down on the ledge.

That wasn't the first time the Trojans had pulled out a win like this during the season. Four weeks earlier, Fertig, Sherman, and Garrett combined to beat California and Craig Morton 26-21 with less than a minute left. Fertig threw a swing pass to Garrett, who went 70 yards down the north side of the Coliseum, putting the ball at about the 20-yard line. Then Fertig hit Sherman with the go-ahead touchdown pass with 50 seconds left.

A number of years later, I appeared with Fertig, Sherman, and coach John McKay along with Irish coach Ara Parseghian, Huarte, and Snow on the TV show *The Way It Was* with Curt Gowdy. I recreated a number of famous USC-Notre Dame plays from the game that morning and later in the day co-hosted with Gowdy in the North Hollywood studio. Clips of the game were shown as the show went on, and I could see Parseghian becoming more and more tense. He was holding the arm rests and his knuckles were just turning whiter and whiter.

They showed the Fertig-to-Sherman touchdown again. In an effort to ease the tension, I said to Parseghian, "Well, you know, coach, they ran the same play in a game against Cal earlier that season."

Parseghian looked at me and finally yelled, "I don't give a God damn what they did to California!" And he just went off—so much so that they had to stop taping the show and resume it after a break. Parseghian was just livid. Apparently, memories never die.

I know McKay always had great respect for Parseghian through the years. He always said that Parseghian might have been the best day-game coach he ever faced. Even if the Trojans went down and scored on their first attempt, whatever they did then didn't work the next time they got the ball. Parseghian could make a team adapt and take the ballgame right away from you—but not this time.

As it turned out, this was the closest Mike Garrett would come to playing in a Rose Bowl. He was a freshman on the 1962 team but didn't get into the '63 game against Wisconsin. He deserved to play in the

Rose Bowl, and the Rose Bowl deserved to have him. It was a shame it didn't happen. When you consider all the snaps he took and everything he did, it would only have been fitting for him to cap his career with a win over a Michigan or an Ohio State in Pasadena.

They called him "Iron Mike," and rightfully so. He had an unbelievable center of gravity, right down to his shoelaces. In the '65 opener, which ended in a 20-20 tie against Minnesota at the Coliseum, Garrett was hit after a handoff deep on the right side. The Gophers' defensive end—I've always had Bobby Bell, one of Garrett's teammates with the Kansas City Chiefs, etched in my mind, but that wasn't the case since Bell had played a couple of years earlier—fell to his knees. Garrett staggered 15 yards sideways as if someone had hit him with a truck. The other guy looked at Garrett with an expression that said, "I can't believe what he's doing."

Garrett, remember, became the first player at USC to rush for more than 1,000 yards (he reached 1,440) since Morley Drury in 1927 (who collected 1,163 yards). Maybe the 1,000-yard mark is commonplace these days, but remember, it wasn't until 1978 that Notre Dame, with all their great runners and Heisman winners, had a 1,000-yard rusher—Vagas Ferguson.

Strangely, one of Garrett's biggest games didn't come while he was playing tailback. In the '65 game at Cal, coach John McKay decided not to play him much in the backfield. All Garrett did was field a couple of punts and run them back through the defense in a 35-0 victory. But one play was so memorable: he ran into a pile that looked like a beehive and easily had 15 players, somehow popped out of it on the other side, and ran 70 yards for a touchdown.

Garrett wasn't as fast as Reggie Bush or O.J. Simpson, but he was so strong, like LenDale White—except that he was just 180 pounds. And to think Garrett almost didn't come to USC out of Roosevelt High. UCLA's Billy Barnes recruited him, but the coach was going to change his offense, and Garrett wanted to be the feature back. McKay heard

Mike Garrett, left, and Tom Kelly pose before a Prime Ticket broadcast of a USC game in the 1980s. *Photo courtesy of Tom Kelly*

Garrett wasn't going to UCLA and sent Charlie Hall to talk him into coming to USC.

Garrett eventually became USC's first Heisman Trophy winner.

And he was every bit worthy of it.

OCTOBER 14, 1967
(NO. 1) USC 24, (NO. 5) NOTRE DAME 7

	1ST	2ND	3RD	4TH	FINAL
USC	0	0	17	7	24
NOTRE DAME	0	7	0	0	7

Quick summary: The previous year, Notre Dame beat USC 51-0 and was a heavy favorite at home, despite the Trojans' No. 1 ranking. USC had not won in South Bend, Indiana, since 1939. Junior tailback O.J. Simpson made his first national splash on TV, rushing for 160 yards on 38 carries and scoring all three USC touchdowns. Adrian Young recorded four of USC's seven interceptions.

John McKay, an Irish Catholic from a coal-mining family in West Virginia, once envisioned playing at Notre Dame. But they gave him short shrift. Apparently, they had enough running backs, so he ended up at Purdue, where he lasted only a year before entering into the service and World War II. After that, McKay came back to play at Oregon under Len Casanova and became an assistant there. He eventually came to USC as an assistant under Don Clark and took over the team in 1960. But I think Notre Dame was always in the back of his mind, and he never felt he got a fair shake whenever he went back.

In 1967, McKay's team was 4-0 and ranked No. 1 in the polls when the Trojans and new tailback O.J. Simpson entered Notre Dame Stadium.

They were in the dressing room waiting for the game to start when an official knocked on the door.

"Time to get your team on the field," the official said.

"Is Notre Dame out yet?" McKay responded.

No answer.

"I'm tired of going out there and having 60,000 people scream and holler at my football team while we're waiting for Notre Dame to walk out," McKay continued. "I'm all through with that. You tell me when they're out there and I'll send out my team."

The official came back a short time later. Same request. McKay turned him down again.

The official came back a third time.

"Do you have a hearing problem?" McKay barked at him.

The official finally said, "Coach, you get your team on the field or we'll forfeit the game."

"And Notre Dame will win?" McKay asked.

"Yes."

"What would the score be?"

"Two to nothing."

McKay thought for a second and said, "That's the best deal you bastards have ever given me." He turned to his team. "Gentlemen, take off your uniforms. We're going home."

Adrian Young, who was actually born in Dublin, Ireland, was beside himself. Here was his chance to finally play against Notre Dame in South Bend. Thinking that he and his teammates were getting back on the bus and leaving, the star tight end was in tears.

Finally, the official came back.

"Notre Dame's on the field," he said.

McKay responded, "OK, thank you. Boys, go out there and kick their butts."

Simpson scored three touchdowns, and USC won for the first time at South Bend since 1939, when Howard Jones and his national championship team came to town. And, with that victory, the game against UCLA at the end of the season meant a great deal more.

NOVEMBER 18, 1967
(NO. 4) USC 21, (NO. 1) UCLA 20

	1ST	2ND	3RD	4TH	FINAL
UCLA	7	0	7	6	20
USC	7	7	0	7	21

Quick summary: USC, which had been the nation's top-ranked team from October to early November, lost 3-0 at Oregon the week before this contest at the Coliseum, giving up the No. 1 spot to UCLA. Not only was a trip to the Rose Bowl and a shot at the national championship on the line, but also the Heisman race between Trojans junior tailback O.J. Simpson and Bruins senior quarterback Gary Beban. Pat Cashman's 55-yard interception return for a touchdown pulled USC even with UCLA in the first quarter, and Simpson's 13-yard touchdown run gave the Trojans a 14-7 halftime lead. Beban's 53-yard scoring pass to George Farmer tied it up in the third quarter and his 20-yard touchdown pass to Dave Nuttall put the Bruins ahead, but Zenon Andrusyshyn's PAT was wide right. Simpson's classic 64-yard cutback touchdown run with 10:38 left would eventually clinch the victory. Simpson, who had just 10 yards on his first 11 carries, finished with 30 carries for 177 yards. USC quarterback Steve Sogge completed just one pass in five attempts on the afternoon, and his backup, Toby Page, who entered the game in the third quarter, was 0-for-1 throwing in the second half. Beban, who was 16 of 24 passing for 301 yards and two touchdowns, won the Heisman Trophy, but Simpson and the Trojans moved on to the Rose Bowl, where a 14-3 win over Indiana, fueled by two Simpson TD runs, clinched the national championship.

As great as Simpson's 64-yard game-winning run was in this nationally televised event, it was his earlier touchdown run of 13 yards that ABC would later use as part of the opening to its college football game of the week telecasts. The cameras may have had a better angle as he was running toward the peristyle end of the Coliseum.

I remember that call: "Ball on the 13 . . . the snap, pitch to Simpson . . . sweeps left . . . gets a block . . . he's at the 10, the 5, touchdown USC!"

Seven players in powder blue had a shot at Simpson but couldn't bring him down. John McKay said, "I don't understand how he made that run, but thank God he did."

This run was overshadowed, of course, by another Simpson run that everyone was talking about. Sprinter Earl McCullouch led the way on 23 Blast, a play Toby Page called as an audible at the line of scrimmage.

A DOZEN GAMES, PLAYS, AND PLAYERS FOR THE AGES

I also still remember the call I made then: "The ball is on the 36 . . . the snap . . . Page turns, hands to Simpson . . . starts to his left in front of the USC bench, turns upfield, he's at the 40, he's at the 45, cuts back at the 50 . . . open field . . . down to the 45, the 40 . . . big-time run . . . at the 20, 15, 10, 5, touchdown! The crowd is going crazy!"

Simpson started toward the peristyle end, swung over near McKay's bench, and came across the field. McCullouch had been spread to the right side.

UCLA coach Tom Prothro, who was not given over to great press statements and was usually devoid of humor, nevertheless had a great line when asked about Simpson's run: "I knew we were in trouble when the only man who could catch him was blocking for him."

Years later, when we created the history of USC video, we put Simpson in a chair and asked him to remember that play. He said he couldn't believe Page called the audible on a play that was originally going to be a pass, making it a run on third-and-8.

But you knew Simpson was capable of that kind of run every time he touched the ball.

The fact is, the more Simpson ran, the better he ran. It may have been because he was a sprinter in a heavyweight's body. Every time a player hit him, he took his time getting up. And every time he hit a player, that player paid for it. At the end of a difficult encounter, the defense was really worn out. He could really put the hurt on someone. Players were chasing him all the time; defensive backs had to run 30 yards to get him.

As this game proved, Simpson was an amazing back in big contests. I don't recall him ever having a bad big game. Garrett had good games, but Simpson had spectacular big games.

Of course, Simpson could have won the Heisman in 1967, though Beban took the trophy home. The only comparable running back at that time was LeRoy Keyes, a great two-way player—he also played cornerback—out of Purdue who finished third in the Heisman race in '67 and second to Simpson in '68.

Simpson appeared in two Rose Bowls and set 19 NCAA, conference, and USC records in just two years. For him to get 1,700 yards in '67 and 1,880 in '68 when he knew everyone was trying to stop him was remarkable. A sprinter with enormous shoulders, he was also part of the 4x100 world champion track relay team.

Simpson was a longtime member at Riviera Country Club; in fact, his locker was next to mine. He played at the club two or three times a week—many times with Marcus Allen, who was probably his best friend outside of Al Cowlings, as his guest. O.J. was an extremely strong hitter who knocked the ball a long way, but, like any great athlete who tries the sport, he sometimes didn't know where it was going. He was also a great card player and a great gin player. Most of the people he played with are gone now.

The whole trial Simpson faced was a terrible time for a number of people and still affects them to this day. Destined to go down in history as one of the most talked about legal matters in this country, it will never be forgotten.

SEPTEMBER 12, 1970
(NO. 3) USC 42, (NO. 16) ALABAMA 21

	1ST	2ND	3RD	4TH	FINAL
USC	12	10	10	10	42
ALABAMA	0	7	6	8	21

Quick summary: Alabama coach Bear Bryant convinced USC coach John McKay to bring his team to Legion Field in Birmingham, Alabama, for a contest that many say changed how African-American players were perceived in the South. USC sophomore fullback Sam Cunningham had 135 yards and two touchdowns on just 12 carries, while the other two African-American Trojan All-Americans, quarterback Jimmy Jones and tailback Clarence Davis, also impressed the crowd.

They call it "the game that integrated the South," but I had no idea going in what impact it would have. Maybe some did, but I don't think many people in Los Angeles thought anything more of it. At USC, we thought of football players as football players. The individuals in this part of the country may have just naturally assumed that black players were abundant in the South. In those days, USC didn't play at Miami, LSU, Tennessee, or Alabama. They never went to Georgia or Mississippi.

Supposedly, John McKay and his best pal, Bear Bryant, spent time each spring in Palm Springs. Bryant played in the Bob Hope Classic. Like any two coaches who needed another game on the schedule, Bryant proposed that USC come to Alabama one year and his team would play at the Coliseum the next. I don't think either would talk about the plan publicly or answer the question, "Did you deliberately do this?" if it were put to them. If they did, I certainly didn't hear about it.

I know Cunningham had a great day, but at least a half-dozen black starters on that great USC team also performed well. I think McKay felt bad that he had beaten his buddy, and was ready to apologize as he crossed the field after the game. But Bryant supposedly said, "Don't you give it a thought. You didn't beat us. We just ran out of time."

What leads me to suspect that this was some kind of planned venture is based on what a few people told me. Realizing the day of the black athlete was coming, Bryant, like most coaches in the South, was unhappy seeing great local black talent go north to play out of state. He may have urged McKay to come out for a game that Southerners would hear about in order to change their way of thinking.

Whether Sam Cunningham made it to the Alabama locker room, I don't know. I was up in the press box. A number of people say Bryant took Cunningham on a walk along the big hallway between team dressing rooms. Many big-time Alabama supporters had gathered in that hall to congratulate the coach, and Bryant supposedly made a point to stop in front of the donors and tell them, "Gentleman, take a look. This is what a football player looks like. This is what football is going to look like in the South. Get used to it." It may have been a not-so-veiled warning that if Alabama was going to compete, changes needed to happen.

I don't know if it's the truth, but it's as good an explanation as any I've read or heard about. I must say that even Sam was hazy about everything that transpired. It wouldn't surprise me if the rest of the players didn't remember much, either. Going from Southern California to Birmingham was a drastic change for them. I think it was almost a traumatic experience.

The following year, Bryant beat McKay 17-10 in the night-game opener at the Coliseum. Coaching opposite each other in little porkpie hats without headsets, the two of them were something.

Supposedly, McKay helped Bryant land his first black star player. They were talking about recruits one day when McKay told Bryant about this great defensive end playing at a junior college in Mobile, Alabama.

"Know anything about him, Bear?" McKay asked.

Bryant replied, "No, what's his name?"

"A junior college player named Mitchell," said McKay. "He's going to be a great player for me."

Bryant supposedly got on the phone, called Tuscaloosa, and asked someone on his staff to check out the kid. John Mitchell became an All-America player for Alabama in 1972, starting all 24 games in his two years with the Tide and leading them to a pair of SEC titles. McKay would later regret telling Bryant about the recruit.

JANUARY 1, 1973, ROSE BOWL
(NO. 1) USC 42, (NO. 3) OHIO STATE 17

	1ST	2ND	3RD	4TH	FINAL
USC	7	0	21	14	42
OHIO STATE	0	7	3	7	17

Quick summary: USC, ranked No. 1 since the second game of the season, rolled into the Rose Bowl with an 11-0 record, having outscored its opponents 425-117. Fullback Sam Cunningham, whose 11 carries for 38 yards were otherwise not all that impressive, dived for four touchdowns, the most in the

A DOZEN GAMES, PLAYS, AND PLAYERS FOR THE AGES

modern era of the Rose Bowl. Anthony Davis ran for 157 yards, and quarterback Mike Rae passed for 229 yards.

It's not as if John McKay didn't want to beat Big Ten teams or win Rose Bowl games. He raised the bar very high for teams and coaches who came out to play on the West Coast. No longer could they think of this event as just a pleasant two weeks of eating at Lawry's, going to Sea World, or hanging out at the beach. McKay really elevated West Coast football. I thought that—and I could be off base here—while he did want to win that Rose Bowl, he treated the game as a reward. Winning was great. It's always great to win. But I don't know whether he ever went into a big funk when they lost.

Yet for some reason, I know that he really enjoyed socking it to Woody Hayes in the Rose Bowl. Ohio State beat USC 27-16 in the '69 Rose Bowl, when Rex Kern guided the Buckeyes to a national championship just a few weeks after O.J. Simpson won the Heisman Trophy. And the year after '73, Ohio State beat McKay's team 42-21, almost a reversal in scoring, with Archie Griffin and Cornelius Greene.

But this year, with a squad that many consider to be one of college football's all-time greatest teams, McKay enjoyed a real beating against Hayes. The head coach sent Sam Cunningham, who had already taken his shirt and half his pads off, into the game late to really put it to 'em, even though the score was in hand. USC got the ball near the 3-yard line and McKay called a time out, made Sam suit up again, put him back into the game, and made a hand gesture to Hayes across the field that Cunningham was going to dive into the end zone again—for the fourth time that afternoon.

Wherever Hayes spit when he saw that, the Rose Bowl grass has never grown back.

NOVEMBER 30, 1974
(NO. 6) USC 55, (NO. 5) NOTRE DAME 24

	1ST	2ND	3RD	4TH	FINAL
NOTRE DAME	14	10	0	0	24
USC	0	6	35	14	55

Quick summary: Notre Dame broke out to a 24-0 lead before Anthony Davis' 8-yard touchdown reception from Pat Haden with 10 seconds left before halftime put USC on the scoreboard against the nation's No. 1-ranked defense. The extra point was blocked. In the locker room, coach John McKay told his team, "OK, in the second half, they're gonna kick the ball to AD, and he's gonna bring it all the way back." Davis took that kickoff 2 yards deep, saw some daylight, and had passed every Irish player by midfield, running the ball back for a 102-yard touchdown. On USC's next possession, Davis capped a drive with a 6-yard touchdown run. After an Irish fumble, Davis again scored from 4 yards out, then added a two-point conversion run for a 27-24 USC lead. Marvin Cobb returned a punt 56 yards to set up a Pat Haden-to-J.K. McKay 18-yard touchdown pass. Charles Phillips made an interception and returned it to midfield, and Haden hit McKay for 44 yards and another touchdown to cap the 35-point third quarter. USC would add two more touchdowns in the first two minutes of the fourth quarter on a Haden-to-Shelton Diggs 16-yard TD pass and a Phillips interception return of 58 yards—making eight touchdowns in 17 minutes. Davis ended up with just 61 yards rushing on 18 carries, but the senior's four touchdowns gave him 11 total in three games against the Irish.

If I had a dime for every person who told me he was at that game, I could buy the Coliseum and refurbish it.

I've often thought how similar this was to the '64 game, though it wasn't such a big contest. USC trailed 17-0, but threatened to score the entire game. The same was true of this game. USC was repeatedly inside the 20, but couldn't get the job done until the end of first half, when A.D. ran around the left side for six points to make it 24-6 at halftime. But this could have easily been a tie game. A few people thought that Notre Dame was just too good, and USC wasn't good enough to keep up with them.

But Davis' second-half kickoff return started what has to be, no matter if you are a Trojans or Irish fan, one of the greatest 15 minutes in college football history. I don't think Notre Dame made a first down in that entire period. It was unreal. No matter what Notre Dame tried to do, they failed.

At one point, Dave Levy, the assistant coach, was on the sidelines and McKay hollered at him to come over.

"Look around," McKay told him.

And Levy said, "Yes, Coach, what?"

"Is this the damndest thing you've ever seen?" asked McKay.

A number of teams had not scored 35 points in seven years against Notre Dame, let alone in one quarter. Every time Notre Dame got the ball, they became more inept. That was the game in which Ara Parseghian wrote on the board at halftime, "Only 30 minutes more for a national championship." It ended his career.

Going into that game, I thought Anthony Davis deserved the Heisman Trophy. He was built up at running back, though he was probably a better baseball player. He and Ricky Bell were two of the Trojans throughout USC's history I thought had justifiable claims on that coveted trophy.

It just so happened that Woody Hayes, the Ohio State coach, was broadcasting the game for ABC on national TV with Keith Jackson. At halftime, Hayes came over to our booth for an interview, and he and I got into a heated discussion about the Heisman Trophy. He, of course, loved Archie Griffin, his man at Ohio State. I kept saying, "Davis is the best running back in the country and ought to win the Heisman." But Hayes emphatically told me no more than once; his man was the best and deserved it. Remember, it was still late in the season and the votes hadn't been counted.

As the ball went into air on the kickoff to start the second half, I said on the radio, "So far it's been a Notre Dame afternoon . . . the kickoff, ball end over end in the end zone, Davis has it a yard deep and he's coming out."

While I recited his run up the middle, behind the wedge, to the sideline nearest the press box, and down the field, I turned my body to follow him. As I kept turning, I saw Hayes in the next booth over—he was looking at me because he could hear my call. Everyone could hear me, even if those people in the first row. Finally, Davis was on his knees in the end zone, doing that shuffle dance he did. And I found myself looking right at Hayes. I would be for the rest of that quarter because every single score was at the tunnel end of the Coliseum.

I swear, by the time that third quarter ended, Hayes had lowered his head below the table. He just couldn't bear to see what was happening. I kept looking at him and mouthing the words "Anthony Davis."

Has any other player been hanged in effigy at South Bend? Only Anthony Davis. The 11 touchdowns he had in three games against Notre Dame was ridiculous. What he accomplished in his career was equally impressive: three Rose Bowls, two national championships, 3,724 yards total rushing, and 44 touchdowns. It was a fitting tribute to his skill. To have that kind of career against Notre Dame was the stuff of Hollywood. That's not to say he wasn't as good against other teams; he certainly was. But he still didn't receive the Heisman, which was unfair.

JANUARY 1, 1975, ROSE BOWL
(NO. 5) USC 18, (NO. 3) OHIO STATE 17

	1ST	2ND	3RD	4TH	FINAL
USC	3	0	0	15	18
OHIO STATE	0	7	0	10	17

Quick summary: USC was in trouble early when star tailback Anthony Davis, runner-up to Ohio State's Archie Griffin in the Heisman race, went out with a rib injury and was replaced by Allen Carter. Coach John McKay's son, J.K. McKay, caught a 38-yard touchdown pass from Pat Haden with 2:03 to play. Haden then hit a two-point conversion pass to Shelton Diggs for the win.

A DOZEN GAMES, PLAYS, AND PLAYERS FOR THE AGES

USC went ahead 10-7 in the fourth quarter on a 9-yard touchdown pass from Haden to Jim Obradovich, but Ohio State drove 82 yards on the ensuing drive for the 17-10 lead. On USC's final drive, Carter picked up a critical first down on a fourth-and-1 play at the OSU 39. Ricky Bell also gained 6 yards on that drive before Carter made three short runs to set up a Haden-to-McKay score. The game ended when Ohio State kicker Tom Skladany was short on a 62-yard field-goal try. Haden threw for 181 yards and the Trojans secured a national championship.

Not only was it the final Rose Bowl for coach John McKay, but it was also the end of Pat Haden and J.K. McKay's three-year USC careers.

Damon and Pythias had nothing on these two.

McKay and Haden spent their high school days at Bishop Amat in West Covina. They were setting all kinds of records back then. You know that Notre Dame, the great Catholic university, recruited both of them. When a writer asked Coach McKay about that, he responded, "Well, one of those kids is sleeping in my back bedroom, and I'm sleeping with the other kid's mother. I think I'm in pretty good shape with those two." Stanford was also interested in the players, to which McKay said, "If it was between Stanford and Red China, I would pay their way to Peking."

How many of McKay's contemporaries could come up with lines like that?

Haden and McKay got a taste of what USC was all about as backups on the '72 team, which went to the '73 Rose Bowl and included Mike Rae, Sam Cunningham, and Anthony Davis. They had that bitter taste of defeat in the '74 Rose Bowl, losing to Ohio State by 21 points. This game, played a month after that 55-24 win over Notre Dame, was their ultimate redemption, and the play to beat the Buckeyes was classic.

If any two athletes were more joined at the hip, they couldn't have been better than these two. Haden lived in McKay's back bedroom during his senior year of high school. They continue to kid each other about how short Haden is, and J.K. will still tell you he was 30 points better than Haden as a basketball player. If their verbal exchanges became too mean, Haden would call a play in which he'd throw it to McKay over the middle. J.K. was gifted, but that was a terrible place to catch a ball. He'd prefer anywhere else to there.

Although he didn't like taking passes over the middle, J.K. did so every year against some of the best players in the game.

In order for McKay to play for his father, the No. 1 show in town and the media's idol, he had to be tremendous. And if you get a scholarship, you immediately have to be like Caesar's wife, above reproach and better than the guy who others thought should have been given that same scholarship. Everyone's first implication is, "Well, he's the coach's kid, no wonder he got the spot." But No. 25 had to earn it. I remember a spring game in which J.K. got banged up near the eye. Coach McKay told his assistant, Dave Levy, that he needed another wideout to join the scrimmage. Levy told him J.K. had a big cut and wasn't available. "He has another eye, send him in," the coach reportedly said. J.K. lived up to the hype and quieted the fears of those critics who said he didn't deserve to be there.

J.K. wasn't a big, physical player. And, of course, neither was Haden.

I never realized how smart Haden was when I interviewed him throughout those years. Maybe his athletic ability overshadowed his intelligence. People who qualify as Rhodes Scholar are few and far between. To be chosen for this magnificent achievement is like winning a Nobel Prize: you're always that specific winner. Our concern in the media was to watch Haden achieve greatness in football. All of a sudden, it was like whipped cream on the cake. What a great way for him to top his career. To play the demanding position of quarterback and then turn around to become a Rhodes Scholar is amazing.

Haden and McKay. Their careers at USC included some of the greatest games in that era. Both went on to become lawyers, working for the same firm at one point in time. And it's common knowledge that J.K. McKay named one of his sons Haden. So Haden-to-McKay continues today.

A DOZEN GAMES, PLAYS, AND PLAYERS FOR THE AGES

JANUARY 1, 1980, ROSE BOWL
(NO. 3) USC 17, (NO. 1) OHIO STATE 16

	1ST	2ND	3RD	4TH	FINAL
USC	3	7	0	7	17
OHIO STATE	0	10	3	3	16

Quick summary: USC's Charles White ran for a Rose Bowl-record 247 yards, including a 1-yard spinning touchdown dive with 1:32 to play. That capped an eight-play, 83-yard march on the ground that started with 5:21 remaining on the clock. White carried the ball six times for 71 yards on that drive. USC was winning 10-0, but the Buckeyes came back for a 16-10 lead in the final quarter.

When Charlie White came onto the field, the fans received as great a performance as they expected out of him. There are a number of games when good players disappear. But not No. 12.

When I was working at Channel 2, someone from USC asked me if I'd interview this running back at San Fernando High, so a cameraman and I went out there. I remember how dark it was. I'm sure not many TV crews would make that kind of trip just to talk to a high school football player, but it turned out Charlie White was worth it.

He was a free spirit involved in many things people his age were involved in, but that didn't mean he couldn't play football. He's the last running back I've seen hurdle a would-be tackler—he just jumped over him at full speed and kept on going.

I'm sure White was hit and hurt a lot, but he never mentioned it. A tough, tenacious runner, he showed plenty of courage in the Rose Bowl against Ohio State that capped off his college and Heisman Trophy career. He also proved his worth the year before in the 17-10 win over Michigan, where he accumulated another 99 yards and scored that decisive touchdown on the controversial 3-yard plunge in the second quarter.

Until just a handful of years ago, White's name appeared at No. 2 behind Pitt's Tony Dorsett on the NCAA all-time rushing leader list. Remember, running behind the likes of Anthony Munoz, Keith Van

Horne, Roy Foster, Brad Budde, and, of course, his fullback, Marcus Allen, he set 22 NCAA, conference, and school records.

I must say that the relationship between John Robinson and him was tremendous. White was drafted by the Cleveland Browns but eventually cut, and Robinson picked him up immediately with the Rams. That wasn't just for show. Between 1985 and '88, White was named the NFC comeback player of the year, running for 1,387 yards and 11 touchdowns in '87.

On the final drive of the '80 Rose Bowl, everyone knew they were going to get the ball to White as much as possible. He was electrifying, and it wasn't unexpected.

I think he even ran off the field once to throw up on that drive. But, as you sat there, you almost knew that he'd get the job done.

White was as good a running back as I've ever seen. It's hard to pick one athlete over another, especially with all the Heisman winners and those players we many times forget to include, like Clarence Davis. Anthony Davis and Ricky Bell deserved Heismans as well, and Willie Brown was a gifted runner. But I'll admit that White is one of my all-time favorites.

NOVEMBER 21, 1981
(NO. 10) USC 22, (NO. 15) UCLA 21

	1ST	2ND	3RD	4TH	FINAL
UCLA	7	11	3	0	21
USC	3	9	0	10	22

Quick summary: In what would be the final year that USC and UCLA shared the Coliseum as their home field, Marcus Allen, set up by a Tom Ramsey pass interception, scored the go-ahead touchdown with 2:14 to play. Yet UCLA had a final shot to win it. Norm Johnson lined up for a 46-yard field goal attempt with four seconds left, but George Achica broke through Dennis Edwards and Charles Ussery to block the kick as time ran out, preserving the win—USC's 11th over UCLA in 15 years—and knocking the Bruins out of the Rose Bowl once Washington beat Washington State. In his last game at the Coliseum, Allen ran for 219 yards on 40 carries.

A DOZEN GAMES, PLAYS, AND PLAYERS FOR THE AGES

In the USC-UCLA game one year earlier, the Bruins held Marcus Allen to 72 yards rushing on 37 carries for a win for coach Terry Donahue, who had lost four in a row. But, as Allen said of this '81 game in our video production of *Crosstown*, highlights of the USC-UCLA rivalry, "It's one thing to end your final game at the Coliseum with a win, because if you lose and have to walk the seniors out, it really puts a damper on things. We walked out the right way." Allen was named the USC player of the game.

Since USC had been upset 13-10 by Arizona and then lost 13-3 the week before this game at Washington, the Trojans needed this victory to end the season tied for second in the Pac-10. At 9-2 overall, they went on to the Fiesta Bowl at Sun Devil Stadium, but fell flat 26-10 against No. 7 Penn State. Allen was held to 85 yards, and the only USC touchdown was a Chip Banks interception return.

Allen later became college football's first 2,000-yard rusher, led the nation in scoring, set an NCAA record for carries in a season, and won the Heisman Trophy. He also led the team in receiving his last two seasons. But that game against the Nittany Lions was not a very good way to end the season.

Allen wasn't just a great football player, he was a tremendous athlete. It never seemed to bother him that his first two years were spent as a blocker for Charles White. He wasn't one of those "Why can't I have the ball?" kind of players.

It wasn't until White left that Allen really blossomed. I'm sure he played hurt, but you never could tell. And he ran as if he had just melted when he was about to get tackled. He could slide and glide better than anyone. Just look at that 74-yard touchdown run he had for the Raiders in the Super Bowl. That said it all.

When he came to USC out of Lincoln High in San Diego, everyone thought he was too quick for his own good. Sometimes, he went one way, stopped and turned, and his feet flew out from under him because he was ahead of his own footwork.

When you compare Marcus Allen to all the other USC Heisman running backs, as well as the great Anthony Davis and Ricky Bell, who set the NCAA single-game rushing record of 347 yards on 51 carries against Washington State in 1976, Allen might have been similar to a Reggie Bush because he was a threat in so many ways. Bush figures to be up among the best, but I can't pick one of them over the others. You'd have to be a genius to do so. Every one of those athletes played as well as advertised.

NOVEMBER 21, 1987
USC 17, (NO. 5) UCLA 13

	1ST	2ND	3RD	4TH	FINAL
UCLA	7	3	3	0	13
USC	0	0	3	14	17

Quick summary: Erik Affholter juggled a 33-yard touchdown pass from Rodney Peete near the end zone out-of-bounds marker with 7:59 to play, giving USC the comeback victory and putting the Trojans in the Rose Bowl. Affholter caught nine passes for 151 yards in the game, while Peete threw for 304 yards. UCLA's Gaston Green ran 30 times for 138 yards, while quarterback Troy Aikman threw for 171 yards—88 of them were to Flipper Anderson.

The game at the Coliseum is most remembered for Affholter's catch. It reminded me of the Gary Beban-to-Kurt Altenberg exchange with four minutes left that led UCLA to a 20-16 win over Mike Garrett's team in 1965, or even the Jimmy Jones-to-Sam Dickerson play in the '69 USC-UCLA game. But I will never forget the play Peete made right before the end of the first half. The Bruins led 10-0 and were holding USC back as the first-half clock was about to expire. On the last play, Peete rolled out and made the critical error of throwing back across the field. The ball was tipped into the end zone and the hands of UCLA cornerback Eric Turner. He decided to run the ball out. By midfield, it looked as if he'd make it all the way across the northern sideline. But Peete, who was no small man at 6-foot-2 and 200 pounds, charged after him on as great a run as any in that great old stadium. Turner returned it 90 yards before Peete caught him and hauled him down to prevent the touchdown.

A DOZEN GAMES, PLAYS, AND PLAYERS FOR THE AGES

Many don't remember that the game ended when UCLA quarterback Troy Aikman and the Bruins lined up at the USC 21-yard line with 1:07 left. USC's Mark Carrier picked off Aikman's pass, sending the Trojans to their 25th Rose Bowl in school history. Peete was a big-time Heisman candidate, finishing second to Barry Sanders. He is very charismatic, and his NFL career defies description. To play so long as both a starter and a backup with all those bumps and bruises, he really was a survivor.

NOVEMBER 17, 1990
(NO. 19) USC 45, UCLA 42

	1ST	2ND	3RD	4TH	FINAL
USC	14	7	3	21	45
UCLA	7	7	7	21	42

Quick summary: Before 98,000 at the Rose Bowl, the highest-scoring game in the series between the two schools ended when quarterback Todd Marinovich hit Johnnie Morton with a 23-yard touchdown pass with 16 seconds left. In a 42-point fourth quarter, the lead changed hands four times. Three touchdowns were scored in the final 3:09. Morton caught a 21-yard TD pass from Marinovich for a 38-35 lead, but UCLA's Kevin Smith scored a 1-yard touchdown to give the Bruins a 42-38 lead with 1:19 to go. Marinovich passed for 215 yards and those two late touchdowns and ran another in. Morton caught four passes for 70 yards. Tommy Maddox led UCLA, connecting on 26 of 40 passes for 409 yards for three touchdowns, but two of his passes were intercepted and returned for USC touchdowns.

This might have been as good a spectator game between USC and UCLA as this town has ever seen. As I walk across the Brookside golf course that they use as a parking lot outside the Rose Bowl, the sight I ordinarily see after such rivalries is fans fighting or shouting at each other. But this time it seemed that everyone was mumbling about what a great game they had just seen. Todd Marinovich and Tommy Maddox never gave up. The long drive, the parking trouble, the ticket hassle... it was all worth it that day.

I also have a copy of a great picture from a *Los Angeles Times* photographer. The shot is of Marinovich, lying on his back after he has just thrown the game-winning pass. UCLA safety Matt Darby is standing over him and offering to help him up. But Marinovich, true to his nature, is giving Darby the middle finger. How much better does it get than that?

Marinovich may have been unappreciated during his time at USC. His dad, Marv, was the captain of McKay's 1962 championship team—he was even kicked out of the Rose Bowl for a major infraction in the first quarter. I don't think the idea was original, but, like many fathers, Marv thought he was going to create the perfect player in his son. Marinovich became a talented athlete, but I think he deserved a better shake than what they gave him.

The hair that peeked out of the back of his helmet was a sign of the times and what they were all about. Just because he had long hair didn't mean he couldn't play. Look at Troy Polamalu. You think he didn't perform well at USC? Appearances are sometimes misleading.

The other issues in Marinovich's life overshadowed every big game he had. He's such a nice kid, and he's very artistic. I think in many ways he just got caught up with outside pressures. Many players in that generation were involved in things that eventually cost them great pro careers.

I just hope that things turn out better for him. I still happen to be a fan of his.

7

FOR YOUR CONSIDERATION

EVERY FAN CAN TELL YOU, chapter and verse, about the greatest games in USC history, including Rose Bowl wins and unforgettable meetings with UCLA. But many others deserve more than a casual reflection. Those who played in such games may be lost among the hundreds of great athletes the school has produced, but they remain a part of USC's heritage. These games never go away, and the impact they continue to have so many years after they were played is amazing.

Here are some that come to my mind.

October 6, 1962
(NO. 6) USC 7, IOWA 0

The Trojans had nearly beaten the top-ranked Hawkeyes at the Coliseum the year before, losing on a failed two-point conversion. This year, three games into what would be an undefeated season under coach John McKay, USC is in Iowa City, playing on a field turned into a quagmire because of all the rain.

Ron Heller, No. 33, leads his team, donned in nice, white uniforms, out of the dressing room and onto the field. He trips and falls in the mud, and every one of his teammates tramples right over him. The game hasn't even started and he's caked in mud. But, you know, he scored the only touchdown of that game and USC pulled out a 7-0 victory.

November 17, 1962
(NO. 2) USC 13, NAVY 6

Roger Staubach and Navy faced the heavily favored Trojans at the Coliseum. I've often thought—and you can check with Pete Beathard if you'd like—that Navy scored a touchdown late in this game. It would have at least given the Midshipmen a tie and perhaps spoiled what would turn out to be a perfect season for USC. I recall the play in which Staubach took the ball into the end zone but had it knocked out of his hands. He watched it roll around until it ended up back at the 1-yard line before Beathard fell on it to preserve the victory.

September 21, 1963
USC 14, COLORADO 0

Bob Six, the owner of Continental Airlines and husband of *The Honeymooners*' Audrey Meadows, was a Colorado sponsor at the time. One of his representatives called me to ask if I'd be a guest at a pregame brunch outside the stadium. So Pat McGuirck and I made the trip and arrived at the hotel in Denver to a huge plate of fruit, wines, scotch, and vermouth—all compliments of Continental Airlines. They put us in a limousine and took us to this party with an enormous spread, including a washtub full of shrimp. It really was terrible that we had to leave the party to do the game.

Mike Garrett, who was starting his sophomore season after spending the previous year's national championship season on the practice squad and sitting the bench in the '63 Rose Bowl, launched his career in this one. Colorado couldn't have had a tougher opponent to tackle.

But Colorado had a strategy. That stadium had the longest grass field you'd ever want to see. Looking down from the press box, I swear Billy Barty could have hidden in the grass that day. Every 5 yards was a mowed strip just wide enough to mark the field. When Garrett walked out there, it looked as if he had no legs—all you saw below his knees was grass. John McKay couldn't believe that the Colorado coach, Eddie Crowder, would try to win that way.

It didn't work. Garrett scored both touchdowns in a game played in the rain.

October 19, 1963
USC 32, (NO. 4) OHIO STATE 3

Woody Hayes' team included Paul Warfield and Matt Snell, and USC had Pete Beathard as its quarterback. The rule that existed then stated if you were in the game, you had to play both ways. Beathard, who was also a star defensive back, got hurt, so Craig Fertig had to go in. Fertig had been taking snaps on the sidelines to warm up, but once in the game, he had to take snaps from a left-handed center, Larry Sagouspe. The first one hit Fertig in the family jewels. Fertig went down, the football came loose, and Ohio State recovered. But Fertig had to stay in to play defense. USC held Ohio State, and Dick Van Raaphorst kicked a field goal for a 3-0 Buckeyes lead. When Fertig came off the field, John McKay motioned for him to come over and put his arm around him.

Fertig later told me that, after the game, his mother said to him, "Wasn't that great how the coach put his arm around you?" He continued, "I didn't have the heart to tell her that McKay had told me, 'If they had scored anything but a field goal, I was going to kill you when you came off the field.'"

October 17, 1964
(NO. 2) OHIO STATE 17, USC 0

This is not one of the games Craig Fertig wants to remember. He threw a couple of interceptions and the Trojans were shut out.

Years later, when Fertig was an assistant on John McKay's staff, he attended a coaches convention in New York and ended up on a couch next to Woody Hayes. Strangely enough, the Ohio State coach was talking about that particular game and how he was able to beat one of McKay's teams.

Hayes said, "It's too bad McKay didn't have a good quarterback. We may not have won."

So Fertig had to tell him, "Thank you, Coach Hayes, but I was the quarterback who threw all those interceptions."

It was not one of his most glorious moments, but it's one that Fertig remembers, to be sure.

September 17, 1966
(NO. 9) USC 10, TEXAS 6

Loyola High graduate Steve Grady, whose dad ran a gas station near USC, became the answer to the following trivia question: Who was the USC tailback between Heisman Trophy winners Mike Garrett ('65) and O.J. Simpson ('68)?

Grady, who coached at Loyola High for many years after his collegiate career, was the star in this game, scoring the only Trojans touchdown—even though the Longhorns were honoring John Wayne that day. Apparently, the people at Texas had no idea that Wayne, whose real name was Marion Morrison, had gone to USC. As a result, the Duke was paraded around in a big limo on the field at halftime with his hands in the air, flashing the "Hook 'em Horns" sign.

But the Duke was saying things other than, "Go Texas!"

FOR YOUR CONSIDERATION

November 26, 1966
(NO. 1) NOTRE DAME 51, (NO. 10) USC 0

The Irish beat the Trojans 17-0 in 1960, John McKay's first year as head coach, and 30-0 in 1961, but this shutout loss was most impressive. Notre Dame's starting center was team captain George Goeddeke. A week before the matchup, during that classic "Game of the Century" in which No. 1 Notre Dame and No. 2 Michigan State fought to a 10-10 tie, Goeddeke suffered a first-class concussion. He was being held out of this contest, but as the score became what it was, Ara Parseghian put him in when the Irish were deep in USC territory, running out the clock in the game's closing moments.

I know John McKay always felt great playing against Notre Dame, even when the Trojans lost. This was more than just another date on the calendar. McKay saw Goeddeke going into the game and called a timeout. He ushered his defense over and pointed out the center.

"See that man?" McKay said. "I don't want anyone to touch him."

All Goeddeke did was make the snap while the backup quarterback took a knee.

November 11, 1967
OREGON STATE 3, (NO. 1) USC 0

A week before the Trojans faced UCLA, they went to Corvallis, Oregon, to face Dee Andros, the Great Pumpkin, who had a great team. At 7-2-1, the Giant Killers were led by quarterback Steve Preece, fullback Bill "Earthquake" Enyart, and maybe five others who later went pro. The Beavers had already defeated Purdue and tied UCLA before facing off against the Trojans.

The only offense either team could generate in the rain and mud this day was two field goals. Oregon State's kick was ruled good, but the zebras didn't put their arms up for USC's attempt. O.J. Simpson still managed 188 yards on 31 carries on that terrible field.

FOR YOUR CONSIDERATION

November 16, 1968
(NO. 1) USC 17, (NO. 13) OREGON STATE 13

The Trojans had to pull off a rally to win this one at the Coliseum, scoring all 17 points in the fourth quarter to avoid what would have been their only regular-season loss. But having won 29-20 with two touchdowns in the final four minutes of a rainy season opener at Minnesota, this was a Trojans team used to making comebacks.

Terry DeKraai caught a 22-yard touchdown pass from Steve Sogge, Ron Ayala kicked a 17-yard field goal, and O.J. Simpson capped things off with a 40-yard touchdown run.

September 19, 1970
(NO. 3) USC 21, (NO. 9) NEBRASKA 21

The Trojans scored with 6:44 left to tie the game up. The Cornhuskers, led by future Heisman winner Johnny Rogers, had the ball at the end but never did anything with it to win. The contest was unbelievable and very disappointing.

Nebraska would go on to win a share of the national championship with Texas, and that tie with USC was the Cornhuskers' only blemish in an 11-0-1 season. The Trojans would only finish 6-4-1, ranking sixth in the conference at 3-4. Ironically enough, 1970 and '71 provided two of the worst teams John McKay ever had. But isn't it interesting how things go up and down?

Tom Kelly and John McKay pose at the USC practice field in 1962.
Photo courtesy of Tom Kelly

November 20, 1971
(NO. 15) USC 7, UCLA 7

Can we call this one of the worst games ever played? In a history of truly great contests, this has to represent the poorest game between these two rivals. Both teams were totally inept. The matchup, again played during one of McKay's down years in which Jimmy Jones and Mike Rae alternated at quarterback and the team finished 6-4-1 for the second season in a row, just sticks in my mind. It was also Pepper Rogers' first season using the wishbone with the Bruins, who were 2-7 going into this one after Tommy Prothro left for the Rams and star running back James McAlister was ruled ineligible.

November 25, 1977
USC 29, (NO. 17) UCLA 27

This was another of those great USC-UCLA games that would be decided, in part, by the officials. The key play on the Trojans' final drive was a pass interference call against UCLA's Johnnie Lynn. The penalty led to a 38-yard field goal by Frank Jordan with two seconds left to win it for the Trojans, who had seen a 26-10, third-quarter lead disappear after UCLA's Rick Bashore led three long scoring drives to give the Bruins a 27-26 lead with 2:51 to play.

I knew of a USC alum in town who was married to a UCLA graduate, which is fairly common despite the harsh feelings that sometimes exist between the two schools. This Trojan claimed that when he was feeling amorous and his wife wasn't, she didn't say, "Not tonight, I've got a headache." She'd say, "Not until you admit that Johnnie Lynn did not commit that pass interference."

FOR YOUR CONSIDERATION

September 13, 1980
(NO. 5) USC 20, TENNESSEE 17

The Trojans were playing before 95,000 at Knoxville in a night game. Eric Hipp, who had already missed a couple of field goals, plus an extra point, hit a 47-yard field goal with no time left to win it.

"My God, he made it," I said as the kick went through.

November 22, 1980
(NO. 18) UCLA 20, (NO. 12) USC 17

Don Lindsey, the USC backfield coach, wanted to kill me after this one. The game's key play occurred when Jeff Fisher, USC's star defensive back, tipped a pass thrown by UCLA's Jay Schroeder. Freeman McNeil pulled the ball in and ran for a 58-yard touchdown with 2:07 left. I said on the air, "I can't believe [Fisher] wasn't better coached to knock that pass down and not tip it up in the air and play jump ball."

At the USC coach's lunch a few days later, Lindsey came up to me and said, "How dare you. I oughta punch you in the mouth for criticizing one of my players." Maybe criticizing the player and criticizing the coach goes hand in glove. But I guess Lindsey acted as any loyal coach would. He and I are still friends to this day.

January 1, 1982, Fiesta Bowl
(NO. 7) PENN STATE 26, (NO. 8) USC 10

When doing the game, I had the impression that everyone's concern was somewhere else that day. John Robinson was a great coach and led his team to a bowl game, but not making it to the Rose Bowl, especially with Marcus Allen, was a letdown. It was only human to factor in everything.

With the talented Curt Warner at running back, Penn State thought it was great coming out West to play. I think Joe Paterno's desire to get into the Big Ten was precipitated by his desire to play in the biggest game of the year, the Rose Bowl. Paterno had a great program, and I don't blame him for wanting to make it to the nationally televised game he saw Michigan State, Iowa, and even Indiana play in every now and then. That may have motivated JoePa to make something happen at College Park.

The 1982 Fiesta Bowl featured a terrible performance by the Trojans, who, unfortunately, looked as if they couldn't care less about being there.

September 30, 1989
(NO. 11) USC 18, (NO. 19) WASHINGTON STATE 17

In his first full season as a starter, Todd Marinovich pulled off what has become known as "The Drive"—91 yards on 18 pass plays. The last 2 yards were gained on a toss to Ricky Ervins with four seconds left. Then came a two-point conversion pass to Gary Wellman.

It's interesting how many names you don't normally think about pop up. Ervins, who parked cars at Rose Bowl Stadium to make a few bucks as a kid, became a star on the Pasadena field at the end of the 1989 season. Wellman, a Randy Vataha-type of receiver, was just a 5-foot-9, 175-pounder who lettered all four years and went on to become a fine high school coach.

I don't want to downplay Washington State, but when you consider how difficult it is to recruit a top blue-chip athlete at Pullman, you know those kids are going to play their hardest against the schools in their own backyards that didn't think enough to recruit them. Beating teams like Washington State should then be automatic, but it's never that easy. It wasn't that day, either, but Marinovich gave one of his very best performances.

8

UNFORGETTABLES: PLAYERS WHO DESERVE RECOGNITION

CONTRARY TO WHAT SOME MAY BELIEVE, the history of USC football didn't start with Carson Palmer's Heisman Trophy victory. Nor are the Heismans won most recently by Matt Leinart and Reggie Bush the final chapters.

With some trepidation, I'm going to mention a few names dating way back to a time that many of you younger members of the Trojans family may not recall.

While they didn't capture all the media headlines, these are players I believe in their own way had a direct bearing on the great athletic tradition that USC football is so proud of, and deservedly so.

THE '60s

Knowing I may be biased, we can go back to when I started watching USC games in the early 1960s.

Take **Damon Bame** ('62-'63), a linebacker who seemed to be everywhere on defense while playing guard on offense. Weighing less than 200 pounds, he couldn't acquire a suit on any team today unless the coach could see into his heart and find the desire of a man who wanted to play for him.

Fred Hill ('62-'64), almost unnoticed as a receiver, had a great catch against Notre Dame as a senior—an obvious touchdown to everyone there except the zebra—and made it to the East-West Hula Bowl once the season ended.

How about **Lynn Reade** ('62)? At 6-foot-2 and 255 pounds, he was the biggest lineman on McKay's team at the time. That was one great season he had with the national champions.

Rod Sherman ('64-'66) never seemed to get his just desserts, but what a tough player. He had a great reception to beat Cal and made that leaping, one-handed grab over Tony Carey to defeat the Irish 20-17. Sherman showed that he had a great sense of humor as well when he presented Craig Fertig, his quarterback at the time of the Notre Dame contest, with a photo of the play at Craig's 65th birthday, reminding Fertig that the play was never called "The Pass."

In the early '60s, linemen like **Bob Svihus** ('62-'64), **Bill Fisk** ('62-'64), and **Tom Johnson** ('62-'63) were standouts. You can toss **Tom Lupo** ('62-'64) in there at defensive end. McKay was able to turn the former quarterback, who played with one leg shorter than the other, into a great defensive player.

Hal Bedsole ('61-'63), another quarterback turned star, never made it to the Top 10 at USC statistically, but he was the prototype wideout for all who followed him to the school. I think that **Pete Beathard** ('61-'63) was simply a great athlete on both offense and defense at home, but an additional quarterback who may have been as tough as ever was **Bill Nelsen** ('60-'62).

While doing a basketball game at the Sports Arena one night, I could hear a real leather lung about 15 rows behind me raising hell with everyone. Nelsen, who was sitting next to me, was obviously irritated by this man. Without saying a word, Bill went up the aisle at halftime and hit the guy with a shot right on the button. The fan slumped over in his seat and never said another word the rest of the night. Bill didn't bring up the incident and I didn't mention it again.

Rod Sherman makes a catch in the end zone on a pass from Craig Fertig in the 1964 USC victory over Notre Dame. *Photo courtesy of Tom Kelly*

What about **Dave Moton** ('63-'65), a tight end/receiver out of Stockton who had a moment I'll never forget? As Mike Garrett took the ball down the north sideline for big yardage on a pass play in the 1964 game against Notre Dame, Moton caught Kevin Hardy, an Irish star tackle, with a cutback block. Falling helmet over shoelaces and turning upside down, Hardy never knew what hit him. To his credit, the athlete got up none the worse for wear.

Nate Shaw ('64-'66), a great defensive back and later a coach under McKay, ranks among the very best at what he did.

Gary Kirner ('62-'63) was another undersized lineman who McKay got to play to his best potential and, at times, beyond it. He was named all-conference both years.

There's also **Troy Winslow** ('65-'66), whose dad, Robert ('37-'39), starred at USC years before. Winslow completed 11 of 11 passes against Washington in Seattle, which still remains a record.

One of the best tight ends ever, **Bob Klein** ('66-'68) teamed with Ron Yary to clear a path for O.J. Simpson. Klein had the highest threshold for pain I've ever seen. It defied description. While closing out his pro career with the San Diego Chargers during a playoff loss to Houston, Klein caught a pass from Dan Fouts that split the palm of his hand wide open. The cut was three inches long, at least a quarter of an inch wide and deep, and very ugly. On the bus to the airport, Klein showed me his hand in a nonchalant manner. It had to have been as painful as anything short of a broken bone, but he simply ignored it.

Earl "The Pearl" McCullouch ('67) teamed with Simpson, Lennox Miller, and Fred Kuller to set a world-record 440-yard mark (38.6 seconds) that stands today. He also escorted the Juice on his 64-yard run against UCLA in that memorable 21-20 win.

If you look back at that come-from-behind victory over the Bruins, you will find that smaller fullback **Mike Hull** ('65-'67) blocked for O.J., and **Pat Cashman** ('66-'67), another big-time player, had a big interception.

And, in a matter of big hits, remember "The Wild Bunch"? They were tougher than even Sam Peckinpah could have imagined. In the cross-town bloodbath of '69, **Charlie Weaver** ('69-'70) hit the Bruins quarterback, Dennis Dummit, with an open-field tackle, the impact of which you could hear all over the Coliseum. **Jimmy Gunn** ('67-'69)

Tom Kelly, second from left, talks to USC players Pete Beathard (12), Bill Nelsen (16), and Hal Bedsole (19) at a Trojans practice in 1962. *Photo courtesy of Tom Kelly*

described it as the biggest hit of the decade—bigger than a 45, a 78, or a 33 ⅓, all standard recorded rpms hits at the time.

How about **Jimmy Jones** ('69-'71) at quarterback and **Sam Dickerson** ('68-'70) at receiver beating UCLA with that flip into a darkened end zone in '69? Just before that throw and catch, Bruins star cornerback Johnnie Lynn received a terrible pass interference call, giving Jones another chance. He made it pay off. Even though he was a floor below the broadcast level at the Coliseum, J.D. Morgan, the UCLA athletic director at the time, let out a roar I can hear to this day.

During this same time, **Clarence Davis** ('69-'70), a great running back who never seemed to get his due, went on to a fine career with the Oakland Raiders that included a Super Bowl win. Jones, Davis, Sam "Bam" Cunningham, and Charlie Young had a hand in the game at Birmingham, Alabama, that changed college football forever—and for the best.

One of the best ever athletes was **Bobby Chandler** ('68-'70). He went on to a great pro career and died much too young. In the 1970 Rose Bowl game against Michigan, he and Jones combined for the only touchdown of the day. When I interviewed him for the *Trojan Gold* video series, Jones said the toss was about 50 yards total. Chandler thought it was even longer. At one time it was recorded as a 15-yard play, but it has since been corrected to about 35 yards.

Coach McKay actually ran Chandler off the field as a freshman. The athlete was determined to leave the university. Only after Craig Fertig smoothed his ruffled feathers and built up his ego did Chandler decide to stay. As a senior, he was McKay's team captain. I guess what I'm saying is that although McKay was a tough guy to play for, his brilliant career was not just defined by great wins, but by the players who starred for him and unanimously praise him when reflecting on what they once accomplished together.

THE '70s

It's tough to look back at teams from the '70s and find individuals who were somewhat ignored by the media, but I can give you a couple.

Allan Graf ('70-'72) and **Pete Adams** ('70-'72) were on the line protecting **Mike Rae** ('70-'72) at quarterback. **Rod McNeill** ('70, '72-'73) came back from a major hip injury to star as a running back.

UNFORGETTABLES: PLAYERS WHO DESERVE RECOGNITION

Charlie Young ('70-'72), the great tight end, will tell you the success of the 1972 squad stemmed from its ability to play as a team in every sense of the word. Many think that year boasts the best football team the university has ever had. I'm not about to pick a favorite. All I know is that I saw them all—the '62, '67, '72, and '74 teams, as well as the Robinson squads of the '70s—and to this day marvel at how good they were.

Artimus Parker ('71-'73), called "T," is also in that mix. Out of all the greats who have played cornerback and safety at USC—Ronnie Lott, Mark Carrier, and Cleveland Colter—Parker holds the school mark with 20 career interceptions.

A couple of plays in the 1975 Rose Bowl win put the spotlight on some other athletes. **Allen Carter** ('72-'74) picked up a critical first down with the game hanging in the balance to set up the touchdown toss from Pat Haden to J.K. McKay. If memory serves me correct, Larry Zeno, a former UCLA quarterback who had USC down 3-0 in 1962 only to lose 14-3, had coached Carter at Bonita High School. With USC trailing by a point after the score, **Shelton Diggs** ('73-'76) grabbed the two-point conversion pass on his knees for the victory.

The fact that Anthony Davis and Ricky Bell did not win Heisman Trophies was a major disappointment for Trojans fans and me during this period. I'm sure I'm partisan—I voted for both of them and to this day think they got the short end of everything. It could have been that Tailback U had been in the spotlight so much that some voters downplayed the records of these two great backs and the head coaching of John McKay.

Vince Evans ('74-'76) and **Rod Martin** ('75-'76) were two of the main players who bridged the gap from McKay to John Robinson. It seems to me that Evans played forever with the pros, and what a story Martin was! Robinson almost had to blackmail the Oakland Raiders to draft the athlete, and now he has more Super Bowl jewelry than you can imagine. He'll be happy to show it to you whenever you ask.

Another project during J.R.'s second stint was **Keyshawn Johnson** ('94-'95), who lasted 11 years in the NFL. His Trojans career started on the practice field as a ball boy. After going to West L.A. Junior College, Robinson offered Keyshawn a scholarship. The athlete starred as the MVP of both the Cotton Bowl and Rose Bowl for the USC coach. He's one of the best-liked players ever to wear the cardinal and gold, and, frankly, a protégé of Robinson. During one interview, Robinson told me that if USC ever played a team from, say, Italy, Keyshawn would be on a first-name basis with half the players.

Before Keyshawn arrived, **Gary Wellman** ('87-'90) and **Erik Affholter** ('85-'88) gave us a moment or two to remember back in the '80s during the Larry Smith era. Some fine running backs almost brought back the glory of Tailback U at that time as well. **Fred Crutcher** ('81, '83-'85) and **Aaron Emanuel** ('85-'89) were there, along with '89 Rose Bowl MVP **Ricky Ervins** ('87-'90) at 1,400 yards.

Another 1,000-yard rusher, **Mazio Royster** ('90-'91), came before **Delon Washington** ('94-'97) and **Deon Strother** ('90-'93), who were both four-year players at tailback.

How about quarterback **Scott Tinsley** ('80-'82)? He was interviewed every year for 13 years as the last USC QB to beat Notre Dame back in '82. And while we're talking quarterbacks, don't forget **Brad Otten** ('94-'96), who tied Notre Dame in '94 and beat them in '96 in overtime to end USC's losing streak with a Rose Bowl win over Northwestern sandwiched in between.

Every time I see **Sean Salisbury** ('82-'83, '85) on ESPN, I'm reminded of the time he suffered that broken leg at Arizona State in '83 and came back to rank seventh in all-time career passing, one spot below Otten and two behind Todd Marinovich.

THE KICKERS

Maybe a couple of kickers need to be remembered for their big moments in the sun or their nights in the light as well.

UNFORGETTABLES: PLAYERS WHO DESERVE RECOGNITION

Chris Limahelu ('73-'74) hit a 34-yarder to beat Stanford 27-26 with just seconds remaining in '73. I can still remember Stanford coach John Ralston with his clipboard clutched to his chest, looking to the peristyle end of the Coliseum as Limahelu's kick traveled the other way and awaiting the fan reaction to tell him whether the field goal was good or not. Ralston also had to endure another USC kicker, **Ron Ayala** ('68-'70), who hit a 34-yarder in a 26-24 win in '69.

In a 27-25 win over Joe Montana and the Irish, the game-winning field goal by **Frank Jordan** ('77-'78) deserves a nod. His kick a year before beat UCLA 29-27. Both made attempts were 37-yarders.

Eric Hipp ('79-'80) may not be remembered by many, but he hit a 47-yarder to win 20-17 at Tennessee in 1980.

Adam Abrams ('95-'98) beat Notre Dame in '97. **Don Shafer** ('85-'86) kicked a 32-yarder with no time left in '86 to win in a rainstorm at Baylor—not an easy place for visitors.

Quin Rodriguez ('87-'90) starred for four years and had his share of success, including a game versus Arizona his freshman year in which he scored all 12 points in a 12-10 win. His last field goal came with 1:11 left on the clock.

After missing a few chances earlier in the game, **Dave Newbury** ('99-'01) beat Colorado in 2000 with a 24-yarder with 13 seconds left. Later that year, **David Bell** ('96, '98-'00) did in the Bruins 38-35 with nine seconds left. It was the second made field goal out of six attempts for Bell, who began the year at third string.

PICKING FAVORITES

Whenever I talk to Trojans fans throughout the years, a couple of questions always come up. The first is, "What's the greatest game you've ever seen?" I hesitate to even mention a few. You can pick one out if you like.

But the second question, "Who was the greatest player you ever saw?" is even tougher. I'm telling you, go buy a USC media guide and find the list of every letterman who has ever worn a Trojans uniform. Start with all the players on the 1962 national title team. Pick out your best two linebackers and defensive backs, your greatest tight end, and your finest offensive linemen. Now try to single out a tailback. You have at least half a dozen to choose from, including five Heisman winners and a few others who could have won it. And now you've got to pick a quarterback?

Go ahead. Choose 11 on each side.

I've been a little foolish in my life. But I'm not foolish enough to tell you the best team or the best game or the best 22 players who've ever worn Trojans uniforms. It's like virtue is its own reward. Watching and enjoying them as both individuals and team players has been enough to satisfy me for over 40 years.

9

THE NEAR MISSES

SOMETIMES, IT WAS TOUGH enough just making it to the games, much less broadcasting them.
Knock on wood, I've never missed one.

PROVEN DEDICATION

The closest call I had may have been after a car accident in 1983.
I had just done a Lakers game for ON-TV, the local pay channel service. They played Denver, but I don't remember how the contest turned out. It was a rainy, miserable Sunday night. I drove my Nissan over to West L.A. and dropped a lady friend of mine off at her apartment after the game. I was coming back down Sunset Boulevard to go north on the 405 Freeway when a Chrysler suddenly came off the hills on the street's right side, turned, and hit me head on.
I was jolted forward and hit the windshield. I also grabbed the steering wheel so tightly that I bent it around the post. Somehow, I never lost consciousness, but I was lying there slumped over the wheel and could feel the blood running down my face. I remember thinking, "I hope my eyes are closed, because I can't see. I might be blind." Finally I opened my eyes and saw nothing but blood and broken glass.

Then another car came toward me. I heard its brakes slam and the sound of a woman's high heels hurrying down the street. I could hear her ask, "Are you alive?" I mumbled something. She said, "Thank God; I'll call for help."

Finally, the fire department and police showed up. They used the Jaws of Life to cut me out of the car and then put me on a stretcher. The rain kept coming down as a cop walked over and recognized me. "Oh, you're Tom Kelly. . . . What are you doing in a mess like this?" he asked.

"I got a bad agent," I said. "Look what he put me into."

At least it made the cop laugh.

I was taken to Cedars Sinai Hospital, where I was put under observation in intensive care. I gained a few scars and lost a couple of teeth, but the worst part was taking a severe belt to the heart from the steering wheel, which created problems with arrhythmia and an irregular heartbeat 30 years later and eventually led to an angioplasty.

I was supposed to broadcast the L.A. Express USFL game on Sunday. Fortunately, I was cleared to do the contest and was able to leave the hospital on Friday. The car I was driving had been totaled, but I had a Buick at my apartment in West L.A.

On Saturday I had to deliver some tickets to Sunday's game to friends, so I was driving again. I ended up at a gas station on Westwood Boulevard. I left the key in the ignition, ordered $20 worth of gas at the counter, filled the tank up, and went back to get my two dollars in change. As I was inside paying for a cup of coffee, I looked up to see my car driving away.

"Someone just stole my car," I told the clerk.

"How'd that happen?"

"I guess I left my keys in there."

"You dummy," the clerk said.

He called the police and they showed up, asking who had reported the stolen car.

"I did," I told them.

"Aren't you Tom Kelly?" the policeman asks. "Damn, you're having a helluva week."

It was the same cop who found me at the accident.

"Yeah, I can't believe it myself," I said.

I rented another car and did that Express game on Sunday.

A week later, I received a call from an apartment manager near USC who had come across a number of letters, papers, and two checks totaling $4,000 made out to me in the corner of her garage. Apparently, whoever stole my car had dumped everything out. An impound lot soon called me to say they had recovered my car. The trunk was empty—my golf clubs were gone—but otherwise there wasn't a mark on it.

Not only was I lucky to get the car back, but I was lucky that I made it to that game.

MORE CLOSE CALLS

I had a few more near misses.

I made it to one USC basketball game at Kansas State just 20 minutes before tip-off because of bad weather.

I also broadcast a San Diego Chargers-Seattle Seahawks game at the Kingdome after Chargers coach Tom Prothro refused to hold the team plane for me. I had to find my own flight up there, but arrived a half hour before the team did. Bo Matthews, a Chargers fullback who also missed the bus from Jack Murphy Stadium to the San Diego Airport for our PSA flight, flew with me on that trip.

My station sports director, Pat McGuirck, decided to go with me on my first visit to Notre Dame with the USC football team in 1961. As we flew into Chicago, he wanted to know how we were going to make it to South Bend, Indiana. I had a friend coming in from Peoria who was planning to drive us to the game, but that Friday night, he called to say he couldn't make it because his wife was ill and had to go to the

hospital. "Now what are we going to do?" McGuirck asked. "Because you don't have to bother going back to California if we miss this game."

"I'll tell you what we'll do," I said. "We're going to Central Station and get on a train at eight o'clock tomorrow morning. That'll get us straight to South Bend, and we'll take a cab to the game. The trains have been running 1,000 years, and it's probably the easiest way to get there."

McGuirck was still worried—come to think of it, I may have been worried a bit, too—but we made it to South Bend.

MAKING CONNECTIONS

One of the craziest connections I had started with a USC basketball game in Albuquerque, New Mexico, on a Thursday night, followed by a game in Wyoming that Saturday. Riley Ridderbush, my engineer, flew with me from Albuquerque to Denver, Colorado. We then got a car and drove past Fort Collins into Wyoming toward Laramie for the game. But as we came over the mountain, we saw that it was snowing—about six inches were on the ground already. We made it to a very primitive airport in Laramie, where I told the guy in charge I had to be in Cleveland, Ohio, by Sunday morning to do a Chargers game and wondered if he had any solutions. He allowed me to charter a flight from Laramie to Denver for $300, telling me I had to be back no later than 10:15 p.m. on Saturday if I wanted to make my connection in Denver.

We did the game in Laramie and, fortunately, it ended in time. I made it back to this little airport, climbed into a Piper Apache, and watched the engines turn over as snow continued to fall. The minute we rose up above the clouds, it was perfectly clear.

Tom Kelly displays a 1986 Radio and TV News Association of Southern California trophy for his work at KNX. *Photo courtesy of Tom Kelly*

The pilot got me to Denver and carried my luggage right over to the plane. As soon as they closed the door behind me, we were off to Atlanta, Georgia, for another connection. Once in Atlanta, I got off the plane, found the restroom, changed my shirt, shaved, and then caught a flight to Akron, Ohio. From there, I had to take the subway from the airport straight to Cleveland. I emerged from a hole in the ground, walked right up the stairs, and saw the San Diego Chargers' team waiting to catch the bus to the stadium.

Dan Fouts, the Chargers quarterback, just looked at me and said, "Where have you been?"

"I could tell you," I replied, "but you wouldn't believe it."

GETTING THE JOB DONE

One of the most memorable game weekends I did started with USC's 1982 Fiesta Bowl loss to Penn State in Tempe, Arizona, on New Year's Day. About 71,000 people were trying to exit Sun Devil Stadium all at once. The problem was, I had to be in Miami the next day for a Chargers game. As I was leaving the stadium, I finally had to jump a curb and go the wrong way on a one-way street. I drove up to a cop and told him that I had to be at the airport in 30 minutes, so he just looked the other way and let me go. I was basically tearing across people's front lawns to make my flight. When I arrived at the airport, I had a friend drop off my rental car while I ran up to the ticket booth, checked myself in, boarded the plane, watched the door close behind me, and flew off to Miami.

That contest has become one of the epic games in NFL history. Rolf Benirschke's 27-yard field goal gave the Chargers a 41-38 victory after 13:52 in overtime. ESPN runs it from time to time—it's one of their classics and one of mine, too.

How could I have missed that one?

10

PEOPLE, PLACES, AND THINGS

CRAIG FERTIG
LONGTIME TV BROADCAST PARTNER

People who understand everything there is to know about football have always impressed me. For the most part, I didn't. I knew you gave the ball to somebody, he ran, and he was tackled. But Craig Fertig, my broadcast partner for 15 years, saw everything.

A play would happen and Fertig would say, "Great block by Ferentine."

I didn't see it. We'd run the replay and, sure enough, I'd notice the block Fertig was talking about. He saw everything from a quarterback and coach's perspective. He ran the gamut. If he said it was a cover two defense and a man was cheating, he picked it up just by glancing at the field. A linebacker could shove a blocker aside, and he'd see it.

And there was never a moment of personal aggrandizement with him.

I'll tell you one of my pet peeves: It's your ball, first down on your own 5, and the other team has nine in the box. Why not call a play-action to the tight end? If he's any good, you're out to the 30. But every time I pointed that out on a broadcast, the team with the ball didn't do it.

"Woulda been a great call, Kel," Fertig always said.

I got the feeling he was thinking the same thing, but didn't want to say it himself.

As a coach, he used to put everything in the right perspective. When he was finally given a shot as head coach at Oregon State (1976-1979), his team suffered a 56-0 loss to John Robinson's USC team at the Coliseum. "My biggest concern was the horse coming on the field so many times, because I thought I'd be responsible for killing him," Fertig said after the game.

Even today, I don't know anyone who has a better grasp of the local high school football scene than Fertig. He knows all the kids playing and he'd be a great scout. We talk about it all the time. Several years ago, he knew all about DeShawn Foster, a great talent up in Tustin, California, who was eventually landed by UCLA and now plays in the NFL. Fertig also picked up early on Justin Fargas when he was at Notre Dame High in Sherman Oaks, California, before he went to Michigan and, later, USC.

I was honored that we were inducted into the USC Athletic Hall of Fame in the same year. And he still deserves his just due. I don't know of anyone more loyal to the university.

MIKE GARRETT
USC RUNNING BACK: 1963-1965
   612 CARRIES, 3,221 YARDS RUSHING (5.3 YARDS PER CARRY), 25 TDS AT USC
   HEISMAN TROPHY WINNER (1965)
KANSAS CITY CHIEFS: 1966-1969; SAN DIEGO CHARGERS: 1970-1973
   PLAYED IN SUPER BOWL I AND IV
   8,049 ALL-PURPOSE YARDS AND 49 TOUCHDOWNS IN EIGHT PRO SEASONS
NATIONAL FOOTBALL FOUNDATION COLLEGE FOOTBALL HALL OF FAME: 1985
USC ATHLETIC HALL OF FAME: 1994
USC ATHLETIC DIRECTOR: 1993-PRESENT

When we did the history of USC football video in 1988, Mike Garrett was obviously one of the featured players. We put him in a chair facing

Bovard in front of the Tommy Trojan statue. I was about to ask him a question during the interview when I noticed he had started to cry.

"Is something wrong, Mike?" I asked.

"No," he replied. "Every time I hear your voice, all I can think about is SC football."

We had to stop taping and start over again.

Mike is a very modest, mild, and unassuming guy. We had a great deal of fun traveling together all those years that he did color commentary on USC games with me for Prime Ticket.

I know he had political aspirations for a long time, and he worked at the district attorney's office in San Diego after his NFL career ended with the Chargers in 1973.

But I'm sure he also envisioned that he'd be back at the university in a major capacity at some point, and he's certainly fulfilled that goal.

Whether he has the knack for picking the right people or what, his coaching selections, with the exception of very few, have brought more and more national attention to the university. And it must be noted that the athletic plant at USC has since grown to include Heritage Hall and the track stadium, new athletic rooms and equipment rooms at Howard Jones Field and, of course, the Galen Center.

Garrett has had a very big hand in all of this, and the success of his teams has been very good for the Trojans.

PETE NEWELL
UNIVERSITY OF SAN FRANCISCO HEAD BASKETBALL COACH: 1946-1949
MICHIGAN STATE HEAD BASKETBALL COACH: 1950-1954
UNIVERSITY OF CALIFORNIA HEAD BASKETBALL COACH: 1954-1960
    NCAA CHAMPIONSHIP TEAM (1959)
U.S. OLYMPIC BASKETBALL GOLD MEDAL-WINNING TEAM: 1960
SAN DIEGO ROCKETS GENERAL MANAGER: 1968-1971
LOS ANGELES LAKERS GENERAL MANAGER: 1972-1976
BASKETBALL HALL OF FAME: 1979

I was lucky enough to have Pete Newell as my broadcast partner on Pac-10 games. To this day, he's revered as a true coaching legend. No matter where we went, people seemed to know he was coming. I don't know how.

One day, we broadcast a game against Don Haskins and the University of Texas-El Paso. Newell and I walked in around 6:00 p.m. for the 7:30 p.m. game, and, I swear, maybe 30 people were waiting for him, all with pencils and papers in hand. All kinds of coaches—high school coaches, junior college coaches—wanted Pete to draw Xs and Os for them. They copied down his every word as if God had come to El Paso.

Although he may have been revered as a coach, he never said he was too busy to talk to anyone who wanted him to draw up a strategy for a low-post offense, a weak-side exchange, or a zone press. If you liked basketball, Pete Newell loved you.

I recall one of the games I did at Cal with Pete by my side. It seemed as if we were about 15 minutes into it when I said, "We've got to have a timeout to get some commercials in."

Newell almost took umbrage to that.

"If my team was coming up the floor, they'd have to be collapsing for me to call a timeout," he said. "No one playing for me called a timeout just to call a timeout."

But I could always get him when I made him look at our press passes when we did games at Cal. His was signed, "Pete Newell, athletic director"—a position he hadn't held at the school since 1960.

"Well, we are a state institution, and we try to keep the budget low," Newell would say.

We were driving through Texas on one road trip in the late '70s when I told Pete, "You know, New Orleans is at the end of this road." I thought he might want to experience some of the nightlife that awaited visitors in the Crescent City.

"Oh, I think the Jazz are playing. Rich Kelley, the kid from Stanford, plays center for them," Newell replied.

We were heading to New Orleans, and he wanted to see a basketball game?

So Newell called ahead to get tickets. The game was at the Superdome, which was so much bigger than the Astrodome that you could put the arena inside of it and still have 100 acres left over for corn.

He got us tickets all right—up in the football press box. The basketball floor was almost a rumor.

"You have a tough time getting these tickets?" I finally asked Newell. "I wonder why they were available."

We did another game together at the Gill Coliseum in Corvallis, Oregon. Pete wanted to head over to Oregon State to see a game, so he arranged for tickets. They put us up in the second balcony behind a post. I was leaning one way and he was leaning another in order to see the game.

"Boy, they went all out for us, didn't they?" I said.

JERRY TARKANIAN
LONG BEACH STATE HEAD BASKEBALL COACH: 1968-1973
UNIVERSITY OF NEVADA-LAS VEGAS HEAD BASKETBALL COACH: 1973-1992
    NCAA TITLE (1990)
FRESNO STATE HEAD BASKETBALL COACH: 1995-2002
COMPILED RECORD: 990-228

Jerry Tarkanian and I were working on USC basketball game broadcasts when we drove from Portland to Corvallis for a Trojans' contest against Oregon State in 1995, back when Rick Barry's son, Brent, played for the Beavers. I knew Rick Barry well since we had televised the ABA All-Star Game together.

"You know a lot of people at USC, right?" Tark asked me.

"Well, I do, yes."

"You know, ever since I was at Long Beach and at Pasadena, I've always wanted to coach at USC," he said.

What he was really asking me was, "What do you think my chances are of ever coaching there?"

It had been a couple of years since the NCAA had levied numerous sanctions and accusations against his program at UNLV, which eventually caused him to resign after some clashes with the school's president. Tark had started his coaching career at several Southern California high schools and then went to Riverside City College and Pasadena City College in the 1960s, so he knew the area well.

We drove awhile longer, and I didn't say anything.

Talking about some of the hot recruits in college basketball at the time, Tark said, "You know that kid, Stephon Marbury, and that other kid, Allen Iverson? . . . Give me those two and three others, and I've got you in the Final Four in two years."

I still didn't say anything.

"And in three years, I'd win it all," he continued.

He was still waiting for me to say something.

"You know, Jerry," I finally said, "what you're saying is probably true. But you bring a lot of baggage with you. From what I know about the university, they cannot risk the athletic program—the football program and the baseball program and everything else—because the NCAA might end up renting an office across from Heritage Hall to check up on you."

Tark didn't speak to me for maybe 60 miles, and I could understand that. I don't know whether he was guilty in the past or not, or if he was guiltier than anyone else who ever coached and won in those years.

We finally did the USC-Oregon State game. The Beavers won 90-89 in double overtime for a great finish. Everyone in the place knew Tarkanian was there. Reporters came over for quotes and fans asked for autographs. Eventually, a young assistant walked over from the Oregon State bench, said, "Coach Tarkanian," and stuck his hand out to introduce himself.

Tark said, "I know who you are, son. I saw you right there on the end of the bench."

The kid's eyes were so huge; he couldn't believe that Tarkanian had noticed him.

"So what did you think of the game?" he asked Tarkanian.

Tark looked at him for about 20 seconds and said, "Don't schedule Mater Dei," referring to the local Southern California high school team.

The coach just collapsed. That was the end of that conversation.

As we walked off to the dressing room to interview Brent Barry, I said to Tark, "You know, if I had a phone, I'd call Washington to see if that Secretary of State job is still open. You're so tactful."

"Well, it happens to be the damn truth," Tark repeated.

THE SAN DIEGO CHARGERS

I hadn't even considered doing San Diego Chargers radio broadcasts, but they offered me a job in 1976 after I did a couple of their exhibition games for Prime Ticket in '75, back when Tommy Prothro was the head coach. The next year, Prothro left and Don Coryell came in, along with two of his top assistants, Joe Gibbs and Dave Levy.

I did Coryell's coaching show on Monday nights for KOGO Channel 10, the local San Diego TV station. In the fall, my typical weekend included doing a USC football game on Saturday and a Chargers game on Sunday. I then flew back to KNX in Los Angeles on Monday to do my radio shows, jumped on a plane headed to San Diego to go to a studio for the Coryell show, and made it home to L.A. that night.

I remember how primitive it was flying on those PSA flights back then. They didn't even have kitchens on their planes. We waited at the airport as the engines turned over until the food purveyors came on board. Just after we took off and made it to 2,000 feet, they started handing out the food. It was the only way we'd get hot food.

Dave Levy, whose football opinion I value, said he'd never seen a better passing attack than the one Coryell had developed. Every time

Dan Fouts went back to throw, he had four different options. And Coryell, who was once a USC assistant, had all the credentials: he was the first to win more than 100 games in both college (with San Diego State) and the pros (with St. Louis, which he coached from 1973 to '77 before leading the Chargers from 1978 to '86).

But do you remember the phrase "hoisted on your own petard"? That's what happened to the Chargers every time: they were injured with the same device Coryell had devised for them to succeed. Fouts would march the team quickly down the field on a typical Chargers scoring drive. Then the opposition would fight against the Chargers' defense for about six minutes. Finally, possession would return to Fouts. This time, it would maybe be three plays and out before the Chargers defense would run back out to the field a minute and a half later.

Eventually, Coryell was so good at getting the ball into the end zone that his defense became worn out, and the team eventually suffered because of it.

Coryell was such a fun guy to be around. After the Chargers won a game in Cleveland at the old stadium on the lake, the team was headed home on a long flight back to North Island. By the time we returned, the press and the coaches were up front and the rest of the players were in the back, awash in beer cans.

Coryell got on the plane's microphone and, with a deep, lispy delivery, said, "Listhen, men, we're tho proud of the way you played, it was just thenthational. Remember, they'll be coming after the big guy [Fouts] next week, so all you guys with the niths and bruithes, get to the trainer tomorrow.... And listhen, men, thanks again and don't violate your bodies tonight." The back of the plane went crazy in laughter after he said that last part.

Coryell's TV show always included a current Charger—a Fouts, a Chuck Muncie, or another player—as a guest, and he'd receive some kind of award. Then we'd show the tape of the previous game. If the Chargers got beat, we never showed the other team's touchdowns.

Every clip was punctuated with me saying something like, "So it was third-and-8 on the 38 when this play happened." Then Coryell would reply, "Look, Fouts, look at him! Oh, Charlie Joyner's got it, look at him!" And the viewers loved it. Why not? It was great fun.

In those days, you couldn't help but love being around Rolf Benirschke, the field goal kicker who won so many games. The inside of his locker displayed a huge picture of a snow gibbon that was so realistic it seemed to jump out at you. The poster said, "We're all in this together." After he suffered the onset of Crohn's Disease during his second season as a player, he returned as an honorary captain for a game against the Pittsburgh Steelers in 1979. Louie Kelcher, this 6-foot-7 giant defensive end who had just broken his leg and was in a cast, practically carried Benirschke out to the field for the coin toss. The stadium went nuts. I don't think I've ever seen a city that loved its team as much as San Diego loved its Chargers back in those days. To witness Benirschke's comeback was something. His game-winning field goal to beat Miami 41-38 in overtime in 1981 was one of the most epic moments in NFL history. Coryell called it "probably the most exciting game in pro football history," and even Don Shula, the Dolphins coach, had to say it was "maybe the greatest ever." I know ESPN Classic continues to run it.

You know, as much as I loved college football, as I did those Chargers games, it took me a while to really appreciate what a magnificent game pro football is. On a college team, there might be 10 great players—though even that could be a stretch. But in a pro contest, out of the 22 who line up against each other on every play, about 15 are as good as you've ever seen play those positions. Watching how they manage a game in the closing moments and how well they play through it all, nothing seems to faze them. In a college game, if the other team is losing in the closing minutes, it's often over. Not in the NFL.

The average college team has 85 people while the pros have 45, but they are the crème de la crème. I didn't have any kind of reference point to compare until I did the Chargers, and it was a real revelation to me.

I experienced some of my happiest broadcasting moments doing those games for the Chargers. I only stopped doing Chargers games in 1982 because they changed stations. John DeMott, a staff announcer at KOGO and then KSDO who had been my color man, wanted to be the play-by-play guy, and I had enough going on with USC and the Lakers for Prime Ticket, boxing and basketball broadcasts, KNX radio, and Channel 11.

But the time I had was well worth it.

LOS ANGELES EXPRESS
UNITED STATES FOOTBALL LEAGUE TEAM: 1983-1985
    PLAYED AT THE L.A. COLISEUM
    OVERALL RECORD OF 21-33, 1-1 IN THE PLAYOFFS

I was working at Channel 11 when I heard about this new United States Football League team, the Los Angeles Express, one day at Julie's Restaurant near USC. I was sitting across from a guy who introduced himself to me as Bill Daniels, but the name didn't ring a bell. Don Klosterman, a man's man and real legend from his playing days at Loyola who I knew to be the team's president, introduced Daniels as franchise's new owner. I made enough small talk with Daniels that, halfway through the lunch, he asked if I wanted to broadcast his team's games. Since it didn't conflict with any other jobs I had—this was a spring pro football league—I was free to do it. Rich Marotta was the color man.

This team had such great stars by the time it entered its second season, including Steve Young, Jojo Townsell, and Gary Zimmerman, that the NFL coveted them. And they were playing against the likes of Jim Kelly in Houston, Herschel Walker and Doug Flutie in New Jersey, and Reggie White in Philadelphia—all these players who "couldn't

Tom Kelly, right, interviews Express quarterback Steve Young, left, and coach John Hadl in 1984. *Photo courtesy of Tom Kelly*

play" in the NFL, but would later become superstars in that very same league.

The USFL's end wasn't unlike that which forced the American Football League to merge with the NFL. One league would draft a quarterback, the other league would draft the same quarterback, and a bidding war would begin.

The NFL had made a concerted effort to kill the USFL from the start, which was too bad. For years, they contended that no one would watch football in January, February, or March. Yet the Arena Football League and the European League play in the spring, and the NFL is a big supporter of both. They've now subsidized the European League as well.

I stuck with the Express all three years, although I may have been one of the few who got paid each week. I can't tell you whether anyone else in the league was as lucky.

Working with Klosterman was a treat. He was a football genius. He drafted Young and Dan Marino in the same year in an attempt to get the team going. No one knew talent better than he did, and no one had more courage than he did after he was told he'd never walk again due to a skiing accident.

One of my favorite experiences was watching Sid Gillman, former Rams and Chargers head coach and Pro Football Hall of Famer, act as one of head coach John Hadl's assistants. Gillman already had this reputation as a West Coast offensive genius. Even at his age—he must have been in his late 70s—he was Steve Young's guru. Gillman would line up on the practice field as a defensive back against a receiver, while Young worked with a center and took snaps. The receiver would take off, and there was Gillman, running and backpedaling, covering him. Then he'd yell out, "Now throw it, son!" to Young—and half the time, Gillman would knock the pass away.

The Express played a number of exciting and memorable games. Those who watched the contests will remember them. How it all ended, with the franchise's finances almost depleted, wasn't pretty. I didn't do the team's last game, which was played at Pierce College. I've closed a lot of acts, but I wasn't there for the demise of that one.

THE DODGERS

In 1963, I stood outside the Scandia Restaurant on Sunset Boulevard, where the Southern California Sportscasters Association held its meetings.

Red Patterson, a former New York sportswriter who, as the Dodgers' vice president, had become the alter ego of franchise owner Walter

PEOPLE, PLACES, AND THINGS

O'Malley, walked up to me and said, "Mr. O'Malley would like a tape of your work."

"Oh," I said. "Does Mr. O'Malley know that I'm on the air Monday through Friday from 6:00 to 10:00 a.m. on *The Bob Crane Show?*"

"Why, yes, he knows that."

"Does Mr. O'Malley know I'm on the air in the afternoon Monday through Friday from 4:00 to 6:00 p.m., including a 15-minute show with Elroy Hirsch?"

"Oh, yes, he knows that."

"Does Mr. O'Malley know I'll be doing 12 USC football games and 30 basketball games this season?"

"Yes, yes he does."

"Mr. O'Malley knows all of that and still wants a tape of my work?"

"Well, yes."

"You tell Mr. O'Malley I'll buy him a goddamn radio."

Five years later, I was at Channel 11, the Dodgers' local TV outlet. The station management was so fearful that O'Malley might move the games somewhere else—although, as a point of fact, he had nowhere else to move them to—that we were doing five specials in the spring to prepare Dodgers fans for the season.

While we were in Vero Beach, Florida, O'Malley said to me, "You'll play golf with us tomorrow." He was very proud of his Safari course, which was famous for its third hole, an enormous dogleg 600-yard par-5.

O'Malley and I paired together while Bob Hiestand, our show's producer, played with Jerry Doggett, Vin Scully's Dodgers broadcast partner. O'Malley gave us all handicaps, but I knew O'Malley wouldn't make a bet he was going to lose.

He and I rode in a cart together, and everything went well until we neared the 14th hole.

Out of the clear blue sky, O'Malley said to me in a sarcastic voice, "Tell him I'll buy him a goddamn radio."

I didn't say a word. I didn't even look at him.

He finally asked, "Did you say that?"
"Well, who told you I said that?"
"Patterson told me."
"Did Red Patterson ever lie to you, Mr. O'Malley?"
"Never."
"Then I guess I must have said that."
Neither one of us spoke another word.

I later told that story to Vin Scully. Afterward, I asked, "Could you have lived with Kelly and Scully doing the Dodgers' games for 40 years? I don't think so."

When I again shared the tale at the Southern California Sportscasters Awards banquet a few years ago, Walter's son, Peter O'Malley, was present. As soon as I began to speak, he started laughing over in the corner.

When I was done, he said, "My father told me that, and I know it to be a fact. I can't believe that whole scenario."

I couldn't either. Talk about being dumb and stupid.

TRAVELER

We used to do a John McKay coach's show at KTTV Channel 11 every Sunday during football season back in the '60s. Ken Grossman, a second-unit director at MGM and a big USC fan, produced the show for us. In addition to the coach, we also had Richard Saukko, dressed in full *Ben Hur* regalia, and Traveler, the white Trojans mascot, on the set.

John McKay always walked into the studio ready to go at 10 minutes to 5:00. One of the first things he asked me was, "How are you and the horse doing?"

It seems that pink-eyed Arabians aren't too smart, but they do know who likes them and who doesn't. And this horse didn't like me. Traveler always tried to bite me for no reason at all. And this horse could really hurt you.

I finally fixed that. Fearing that he'd someday take my hand off, I brought a couple of apples to the set. I slipped him an apple every once and a while, and he was ever so gentle then.

ELROY "CRAZYLEGS" HIRSCH
LOS ANGELES RAMS PLAYER: 1949-1957
    CAUGHT 387 PASSES FOR 7,029 YARDS AND 60 TOUCHDOWNS
RAMS GENERAL MANAGER/ASSISTANT TO THE TEAM PRESIDENT: 1960-1969
PRO FOOTBALL HALL OF FAME: 1968
UNIVERSITY OF WISCONSIN ATHLETIC DIRECTOR: 1969-1987

Whenever anyone mentions the Rams, even now that they've moved from the Coliseum to Anaheim to St. Louis, the names Elroy "Crazylegs" Hirsch, Bob Waterfield, Norm Van Brocklin, and Tom Fears are still etched in the memories of Los Angeles football fans.

Hirsch was a man's man. I also met Waterfield and Van Brocklin, but Hirsch was so nuts when it came to his old team that he referred to his son Winn as "Ram."

As the Rams' general manager, he joined me for a show at KNX radio at 5:30 p.m. every weekday for about four years until I left for Channel 11 in 1966. We hit it off right away, perhaps because we had a Wisconsin connection.

Considering that KMPC, which was right down the street, did the Rams' games with Bob Kelley, it was quite a coup for our station to get him on the air.

Each show, Hirsch and I had 15 minutes to talk about anything that was going on in sports. The program was slanted toward football even in July, but we had great writers and we also covered the Dodgers, Angels, and a number of other teams. The ratings were great, and we won some Golden Mike awards.

Every day, the opening of the show started with the Rams' theme song. I'd follow with a recreation of an old Rams broadcast call: "Waterfield up under center, takes the snap, drops back, gonna throw,

Tom Kelly, left, poses with a 1964 Radio and TV News Association of Southern California award with KNX sports director Pat McGuirck, center, and Elroy "Crazylegs" Hirsch, right. *Photo courtesy of Tom Kelly*

looks downfield, has his man open, Hirsch is there, ball's in the air, Hirsch has got it, touchdown Rams!" Then the music swelled.

Sports director Pat McGuirck, who, considering he had gone to Stanford, had a great sense of humor, once had the idea to record a slightly different opening. We put this on the tape before the next show. As always, Hirsch came in ready to go at 5:15, but what he didn't know is that we had set the clocks ahead. Although they read 5:30, it was really 5:28. The engineer punched up the new intro: "Waterfield up under center, takes the snap, drops back, looks downfield, has his man open, Hirsch is there, ball's in the air . . . oh [bleep]! He dropped the damn thing!"

Elroy looked up from his script, looked at me, and looked at the clock. His reaction was priceless. He couldn't even speak. It took him about two weeks to forgive us for doing that.

But we weren't the only ones who gave him a hard time.

George Allen coached the Rams under Hirsch's regime. I hate to say this about Allen, but he was also a politician and finagler.

One day Hirsch came in to do the show, sat down, and muttered, "I can't believe it." He had just come from the Rams' offices near Rancho Golf Course.

"What's that?" I said.

"The secretary just walked into my office and asked, 'Do we owe $600 to Eddie Meador?'" Hirsch said. Meador, a great defensive back out of Arkansas, played for the Rams.

Hirsch replied that he didn't think they owed Meador any money, so he called Allen, who had been responsible for putting in the request. Allen told Hirsch, "Well, I told Eddie if he got me a couple of interceptions in the last game, I'd give him $300 apiece, and he had two of 'em."

Hirsch said, "I told George, 'Don't you realize we spent all summer renegotiating his contract? And now, against league rules, you want me to pay him $600 for two interceptions?'"

I asked Hirsch, "So what happened?"

He said, "Well, you have to understand that Meader was sitting in Allen's office while this phone conversation was going on. And when the conversation ended, and I told him we wouldn't pay it, George turned to Eddie and said, 'Well, I tried, but they just don't want to do it.'"

Those were the kind of problems Hirsch had to deal with.

TOM HARMON
UNIVERSITY OF MICHIGAN HEISMAN TROPHY WINNER: 1940
COLLEGE FOOTBALL HALL OF FAME: 1954
LOS ANGELES RAMS PLAYER: 1946-1947

Another great friend from my days at KNX was Tom Harmon, one of my favorite golf partners. We almost won the "Swinging Bridge" member-guest tournament in Bel-Air one year.

When he was a great two-way player and Heisman Trophy winner at Michigan, I was just a kid in Minnesota. I always told him that my dad used to take me to see him play, and Michigan never beat Minnesota when he was there—which, of course, I kidded him about all the time.

When he was running all over the place with the Wolverines, the Minneapolis newspaper once ran a picture of Harmon standing with his hand on his hip at Memorial Stadium in Minneapolis. His No. 98 jersey torn up, he was covered in mud and wearing his high-top shoes. The headline said, "Minnesota 7, Michigan 0."

His wife, actress Elyse Knox, took that picture and even had a portrait painted of it. It must have been five feet tall. The portrait hung in their home in Beverly Hills, which was once owned by the famous silent movie actress ZaSu Pitts, and was a reminder of the game in which Harmon gained more yards than the entire Minnesota team. The Wolverines had the ball on the 5-yard line on fourth down. Harmon ran to his left, cut back, slipped in the mud, and fell down to end it—that's when the picture was taken.

Once while I was in the office at KNX, Forest Evashevski, the great Michigan quarterback whose job it really was to block for Harmon on that play, came for a visit. Harmon walked into the office and Evashevski was right behind him.

Tom Kelly, right, and Tom Harmon pose during a golf tournament. *Photo courtesy of Tom Kelly*

I said, "Hold it. Stop right there. . . . You two go back out. Forest, you come in front of Harmon. He was never ahead of you."

Forest thought that was pretty funny, but Harmon didn't speak to me a week.

As the first NFL draft pick out of college, Harmon signed a huge contract to play for George Halas and the Chicago Bears, but he decided that he didn't want to play pro football before he went into World War II with the Army. He had already starred in his own biopicture, *Harmon of Michigan*, and wanted to try acting. After the war, he said he'd play for the Rams in Los Angeles. Before he signed, though, he wanted to make a deal in order to pay Halas back for the bonus the coach once gave him. He had already spent the money on his parents, so he paid off the debt by playing.

We really had a great staff at KNX, including Harmon, Tom Hanlon, Bruce Rice, and me. Harmon later moved to Channel 5, and I went with him. I then left for KNX-TV Channel 2 with Jerry Dunphy and Gil Stratton.

Harmon was such a good friend, and we had lots of fun kidding each other.

He and I were actually going to broadcast the Masters together one year. Harmon's daughter was married to the guy who ran the Delco Remy division of General Motors, a big sponsor for national ABC radio. Harmon did broadcasts for the station, and I filled in for him on the weekends.

We planned to leave the Sunday before the tournament. We would stay there all week, then play the course ourselves with the media after it was over on Monday. I came in to do a show on Saturday, the day before we were supposed to leave, when Harmon said that we couldn't go. He was told that we had said something on the air that the people at Augusta didn't like.

"What'd we say?" I asked.

"I don't know," he said. "They wouldn't tell me. But I've got a call into Ben."

There was only one Ben—Ben Hogan, who Harmon was very close with. In fact, a picture of Harmon and Hogan sitting in a cart together now hangs by the members' locker room at the Bel-Air Country Club by the members' locker room.

The next day, Harmon called me at home and told me that even Ben Hogan couldn't get us in. Harmon couldn't believe it. He had national clout, yet wasn't allowed to do his radio show there.

We'll never know what we said, but the people who run the Masters now seem to operate the same way. You know that Jack Whitaker and Gary McCord have been kicked off the telecast in recent years. If you say one thing that bothers the organizers, you're gone. I guess they're still that strict.

That was the only time I've ever been near Augusta.

LET'S MAKE A DEAL

I played at the Andy Williams Pro-Am golf event in La Costa with a couple of guys from Iowa who had paid their way in, and they remembered my name from the time I was a broadcaster in Des Moines in the 1950s. After the match, I sat down with them and their wives.

Into the bar walked Monty Hall, who said, "Hey, Tom, how are you?"

One of the fellow's wives was so impressed that I knew Monty Hall that she asked if I could arrange for a picture with him. Monty, who always had a great sense of PR, posed with the couples, and I took the pictures. He couldn't have been nicer.

As he was leaving, Monty asked me if I could do something for him. He wanted me to come to the ABC TV studio over on Prospect and Sunset, where he was taping *Let's Make A Deal* on Monday night. So after I finished my 6:15 p.m. show for KNX radio, I headed over to find the studio with an audience already in its seats. They taped two episodes of the show on Monday and Tuesday, and two more on Wednesday to fill out the week and beyond.

Monty introduced me to the audience, and some recognized me. He wanted me to do a couple of "test run" deals with the contestants. It turned out that he was trying out some broadcasters in the business to find a backup since he was occasionally out of town doing fundraisers for his Variety Club Children's Charity.

Around the same time, sports announcers Vin Scully and Dick Enberg were also being hired as game-show hosts. I think that sports announcers, for the most part, are used to being relegated to their own devises and need to think on their feet. They have to be bright and entertaining and need to know how to ad lib. When a third-and-8 play is coming up and all of a sudden a couple of guys are injured down on the field, you have to fill the time. Maybe that's why people thought that announcers would make the best possible game-show hosts. Monty Hall himself was a soccer broadcaster who came down from Canada to the U.S. to work.

Monty did *Let's Make A Deal* on and off from 1963 to 1990 and was the producer and executive producer throughout most of that time. I knew the show well enough, and I was his replacement for a couple of years. I also did a couple of pilots, one called *Anything Goes* and another called *Carnival,* for Monty and Steve Hatos, but they didn't go anywhere.

Truth be told, hosting *Let's Make A Deal* was about the toughest job you could have as far as game shows were concerned. First, you had to work with the audience, which was behind you the whole time you faced the stage and its prizes. The way the show was run was also very difficult. I know Bob Barker did *The Price is Right* for many years, but he just had to ask five people, "How much is this armoire worth?" And *Wheel of Fortune*'s Pat Sajak watched as someone else shouted, "Any L's?"

When you walk onto *Let's Make A Deal,* the first thing you have to keep track of is how much cash you have in each of your pockets. The person who wrote many of the deals and met with me before each show would say, "OK, here's $400. Put that in your left pocket. Here's $200. Put that in your right pocket. Here's $150 to put in your jacket." Then you stepped out on the stage to see all these people dressed in costumes. Once, a 50-year-old guy was wearing nothing but a tablecloth as a giant diaper. His wife was wearing two of them, and they were holding a giant baby bottle. I wondered, "These people got dressed like this, got into their car, drove on the freeway, and here they are?" I didn't know what to say to them.

You picked out two people and said, "I've got $200 here, or you can have what's behind door No. 1, where Carol is standing. . . . Or wait! What you don't take, I'll give to those two people over there." Then the first two contestants decided what they wanted to do, and you moved on to the next deal. Depending on which option was chosen, you had to create another scenario.

It wasn't all scripted, and it was tough to keep everything straight. Nothing happened until the MC said so. No one was better at doing it than Monty Hall.

Then, as the last commercial break was being taken before the final big deal, the person backstage would come back over to me and take all the money back out of my pockets. "OK, you should have $300 in your left pocket and $200 that you didn't give away in your right pocket." He was on top of his game.

Since the show isn't on the air any more, I can reveal a little tip: when it came to the end of the show in which two people traded in their winnings for one of the three doors, the only way the MC knew which of the doors contained the big deal was by checking how many fingers the cue-card man was holding up. That was the signal, and not one contestant ever caught on to it.

MEET THE PRESIDENTS

I haven't met all of them. But will Harry Truman, John F. Kennedy, and Bill Clinton do?

I was standing in the rain on a dismal, cold afternoon in Duluth, Minnesota, in 1948 when I saw Truman on the back of a railroad car on a whistle stop. It was already assumed then that Thomas Dewey was going to be named our next president, but there I was, holding a microphone for WEBC. When your bosses handed you a microphone and told you to go out—even if you were the sports reporter—you had to do what they wanted. I walked up and said something to Truman, and he replied, "Son you'll have to excuse me, because I'm gonna give 'em hell." I never got that interview. He walked up to a platform around which maybe 300 people were waiting to hear his speech. I was thinking, "How is this man going to make it to the presidency?" But it turned out he had charisma and was a no-nonsense kind of guy. I thought Truman might have been as good a president as any in the difficult times this country has faced throughout the past 60 years, although he left the White House no richer than when he went in.

In the late '50s, I was working at WMBD in Peoria, Illinois, when John F. Kennedy stopped by during his campaign—again, he was a charming young man, but many thought he'd lose to Richard Nixon anyway. I thought I'd vote for him, but that it wouldn't do him any good. Kennedy, who ended up carrying the state in the 1960 election, was making a speech at the Caterpillar plant.

Kennedy came by our station to record another speech he was giving later in the day. When I walked into the lobby at about 8:00 p.m., the receptionist told me that Kennedy was in the building. Just then, he walked out a door and into the lobby. I, being the bashful type, introduced myself, and we talked sports—his love for them and past injuries—for about 15 or 20 minutes.

You really find yourself in awe of people like that. When you come right down to it, they're on a different level. When you meet them, you don't know what to say to them.

That wasn't the case when Bill Clinton came to Riviera to play golf with UCLA chancellor Charles Young and O.J. Simpson once in the early '90s. Secret Service men lined the entire rim of the course, holding their high-powered guns. On the second hole, Clinton hit into a bunker alongside the practice green where I happened to be. So, as the group was coming up the fairway, I walked over. A couple of guys in suits came right up to me to check me out, but Mr. Young cleared the air and said hello to me, which seemed to calm them down. I told the president, "That's a free drop area where you hit into. You can take the ball out and drop it two club lengths no near the hole."

Clinton gave me one of those looks like, "Who are you to give me the rules?" but then he laughed and said, "Well, OK."

As I understand it, he took a free drop whenever he was playing anywhere.

That reminds me of a time back in the mid '50s, when a fellow named Bob Michaels, from the congressional district in Peoria, was the Republican Whip in the house. He had attended Bradley University, and he and I were friends because of my association with Bradley basketball. When Bradley went to the NIT in New York, Michaels came up to watch the game. He always envisioned running for an Illinois Senate seat. "When I do that," he told me, "you run for Congress out of this district, and I guarantee you'll be elected." I didn't really want to tell him I was of a different political persuasion. The plan was predicated on the assumption that the current senator living in Canton, Illinois, would quit, but he never did. So Michaels stayed in the House.

Maybe it was a passing fancy at the time. Having done all the broadcasting at Bradley, my name was certainly recognized, and Bradley was at the hub of that congressional district. It's one of those things that could have happened that I've wondered about over the years. When he said that to me, I wasn't bashful about considering it. Who knows? I supposed I could have run for the office and given 'em a little hell.

ON COURSE WITH HOPE, FONDA, SINATRA, MARTIN, MATHIS . . .

I'm lucky enough to have had several pictures taken of me interviewing Bob Hope because of my KTTV Channel 11 involvement with some of his charity events at March Air Force Base.

I also had the chance to play nine holes with Henry Fonda at a police benefit in Encino. I was just in awe of Fonda. I asked him about his game, and he said he'd never played. I was thinking right away, "This is a guy who's trying to make a bet." But he wasn't sandbagging. I took him to the pro shop and picked out a set of clubs and a dozen balls for him to use—by the time we were finished, I think he only had one ball left. I was meticulous, counting every stroke, but he couldn't have been more of a crowd-pleasing man. And the end of the nine holes, he thanked everyone, made a joke about us putting up with him, got in his limo, and left.

But the most interesting experience I had was broadcasting the one and only Frank Sinatra Open in 1963, a PGA event that Frank Beard won. In those days, it was almost a given that every big-time singer—Bing Crosby, Dean Martin, Andy Williams—had his own golf tournament. Sinatra had his at the Canyon Country Club in Palm Springs, which was renamed Indian Canyons Resort after Amy Alcott had a big hand in redesigning it.

My Sinatra story starts with Mal Klein, the general manager at Channel 9, who called me at KNX radio to ask if I played golf. I told him I did, and he asked if I was interested in doing the tournament. He only wanted to televise Sunday's final round, but I was more than happy to do it.

I was at the course checking things out on Saturday night when Sinatra came walking by, surrounded by the Tucci brothers, who had played football at USC years before and ran a restaurant in the San Fernando Valley. At 6-foot-4 and 240 pounds each, they were like two

Tom Kelly, right, does an interview with Bob Hope in the mid-1960s during an appearance at March Air Force base. *Photo courtesy of Tom Kelly*

giant pillars on either side of Sinatra. As the group came past me, I stepped up to shake Sinatra's hand and suddenly, Sinatra wasn't there. These two guys had collapsed in front of him. Talking to the back of these two guys' heads, I said, "Excuse me, Mr. Sinatra, I'm Tom Kelly and I'm doing your tournament today. I just wanted to say hello and find out if there was anything you wanted me to do."

Everything just stopped as the two guys parted. Sinatra put his arm around my shoulder and said, "Palie, what is it you need?"

I thought, "My God, I've just had a visitation."

We ended up at the platform behind the 18th hole, where we met Jill St. John and Sammy Davis Jr. All I could think to myself was, "If this thing collapses and we all perish, will I be referred to as 'an unidentified local sports announcer'?"

You have to remember that I hadn't lived in L.A. that long before this, and I'd never seen someone like Sinatra up close. It was a kick. I had a ton of his records, and he was a great actor as well. If anyone captured whatever it was back in those days, he did.

Dean Martin was also there for the event, broadcasting the 17th hole.

I don't think Martin was ever given his just acclaim as a singer. He had a gorgeous voice. Sinatra billed himself as a saloon singer, but Martin could flat-out sing. I later got to know Martin when he was a member at Riviera. He was so popular. Riviera wasn't known for as many of the big-time names as Bel Air was. Lakeside had Hope, Crosby, and Johnny Weismuller. We have had some celebrities at Riviera, but none were bigger or nicer than Martin. Not a member there would ever say anything bad about Dean Martin.

I've been a Riviera member since 1964 and have played with many of the celebrities here. Someone I've been able to play with a number of times over the years is Ken Howard. Although he's more commonly known for his role in *The White Shadow*, he is a bona fide stage actor.

Johnny Mathis is also fun to be around. He was at Riviera for the last Nissan Open, playing in the Pro-Am, and got a kick out of how much of a hit he was. Everyone wanted his autograph and no one was really interested in the pro they were with.

Vic Damone is another one of Riviera's great members, as are Peter Falk, Larry David, Paul Michael Glazer, and James Sikking (who's better

PEOPLE, PLACES, AND THINGS

known as Lt. Howard Hunter on *Hill Street Blues* and Doogie's father on *Doogie Howser M.D.*).

My usual group consists of Lenny Licotta, once a telephone executive; John Tennant, a Scotsman who came here and made a fortune as a real estate builder; Danny Greene, a film editor who worked with Robert Wise and some great movie people and still teaches classes for the International Film Institute; Jerry Butz, a Stanford grad and truly generous man who does motivational speaking; and Dave McKenzie, an attorney for several trust funds—all connected with the Teamsters. McKenzie doesn't own a shirt you can't read, and most are dedicated to the memory of James R. Hoffa. I also get to marvel at Dennis Watson, a South African who is trying to make it back on the senior tour, on the practice green.

We don't play for much money. We mostly play for fun as dream about the days when everything we hit went in the hole.

I must also mention here the name of a great friend no longer with us: Lou Zela, a USC grad who was perhaps my closest friend outside the broadcast world and the one responsible for my joining Riviera.

You know, golf really is an avocation. To those who aren't too athletically gifted, golf is very fun to play. Anyone at any age can still play the game well. Golfers are a different breed. It's tough and people may make fun of it, but it's the only game in which you have no one to blame but yourself. No one dropped a pass, missed a block, took a shot that rolled off the rim, or held onto ball when you were wide open. You keep hitting until you put it in the hole. And if you say you took five strokes when you really took seven, you know you're lying—even if no one else does.

When you think of drug testing and everything else that goes on in this day and age, the integrity of the game is very important. I admire tennis players' skills, but whether you play at Wimbledon center court or Arthur Ashe Stadium in New York, you see the same dimensions and measurements. In golf, whether you're playing at Rancho Park or

Pinehurst, every course is different. Even the worst golf course has a bit of charm about it.

I've had some success. I've hit seven holes-in-one. I've aced every par-3 at Riviera, including the 14th hole twice. Once I even shot a 69 at Riviera. It was the best I've ever done. I made the first ever hole-in-one at Rustic Canyon on the uphill par-3 15th. And, at Huntington Beach's SeaCliff, I aced the ninth hole.

I'm a big fan of the game and am fortunate to still do several golf TV shows. Lately, some of my most recognized shows have been golf shows. People say that they still watch *Golf the West*, and they continue to ask me how they can appear on that show. It's been a running gag between Andy Thuney, the head pro at Hacienda Golf Club, and me. We laugh because I haven't done one of those in years. Another show I've been doing lately, put together by Darrell Rutter in Portland, Oregon, is a team event series. The show features 15 three-person teams, consisting of a head pro, a male champion, and a female champion. Each team represents its own course as the players participate in a series of matches, playing nine holes with the best ball. We did 42 shows in the series, and it's been well received. Golfers are by and large pretty good people who get a big kick out of being on TV.

TOM KELLY, MOVIE STAR

About an hour into the *The Godfather, Part II*, the 1974 Academy Award-winning Best Picture, a three-minute scene takes place in which Michael Corleone (Al Pacino) visits the home of Hyman Roth (Lee Strasberg) for a meeting. Roth is watching a football game on TV: USC vs. Notre Dame—and my voice is doing the play-by-play.

This is the scene in which Roth, who talks about his love of football, says the famous line, "I loved baseball ever since Arnold Rothstein fixed the World Series in 1919." At one point, Roth turns up the TV volume to drown out their secret conversation as Corleone tells Roth, "I came here because there's gonna be more bloodshed. . . . I want you to know about it before it happens." In the background, my voice is heard saying such things as "Pickup of 2 . . . second-and-8 for USC at the Trojan 38-yard line."

Howard Koch, who produced the Academy Awards for TV, put that scene together. I used to see him at the racetrack with Dr. Bob Kerlan all the time while I was working at KNX Radio. Howard called me one day, wondering if I could recreate a football game for him involving USC and Notre Dame. I told him it was no problem. He wanted about five minutes from the game broadcast at the Coliseum in 1953 recorded on a quarter-inch tape.

You get the impression that the game is on TV, but it's really a radio call.

At the USC sports information office, they now keep a very detailed play-by-play sheet of every game the Trojans have ever played.

It might say, "Saturday, September 15, 1958. Temperature: 62 degrees. Weather: Clear. Field: Dry. Notre Dame wins toss and elects to receive. Johnson kicks off for USC. Smith takes it at the 4 and runs it to the 8. . . . "

So I found the play-by-play sheet for that exact game, went into a booth at KNX, asked an engineer to play some crowd noise, and put something together. I began with, "Good afternoon and welcome to the Coliseum," and did five minutes in which both teams scored. I didn't know what movie the tape was for until after I finished it, put it into a brown envelope, and delivered it to Paramount studios.

I received a check for $5,000 and have gotten residuals throughout the years.

Other movie and TV appearances I've made over the years include: calling a football game in the 1984 movie *Against All Odds*, directed by Taylor Hackford and starring Jeff Bridges and Rachel Ward (the football players actually used uniforms from the USFL L.A. Express team); playing the role of a sports announcer in the 1990 John Frankenheimer-directed movie *The Fourth War*, starring Roy Scheider; playing myself as a TV sports-talk roundtable host in the 1994 movie

The Scout, with Albert Brooks and Brendan Fraser; playing a TV announcer in a 1967 episode of the TV show *Batman*; a 1967 episode of a TV show called *Cowboy in Africa*; a 1974 episode of the TV show *Here's Lucy*; a 1984 episode of the TV show *The Fall Guy*; and a 1993 episode of the TV show *Boy Meets World*.

OH, THE PLACES YOU'LL GO

I'll preface this again by saying that I never planned to be an announcer. I went to school hoping to major in English and somewhere down the line go to law school and become a lawyer. But I never envisioned spending 60 years of my life talking in front of a microphone or camera. It was the furthest thing from my mind. So almost every job I've had has been a surprise, I guess.

Weird jobs in weird places?

How about broadcasting a high school football game on top of a bakery truck in Hurley, Wisconsin? Hurley, a city of 5,000 between Northern Wisconsin and Upper Michigan, was playing Ironwood, with whom they had a kind of USC-UCLA rivalry—the two cities were literally separated by a stream you could step across called the Montreal River. But what really separated the two cities was the fact that Hurley had 100 saloons with houses of questionable background above them. While Ironwood was an industrious, modern little city, Hurley was a popular place for iron ore miners and loggers who needed to let off steam. To this day, men go down some 4,000 feet to dig ore out of the ground in that part of the world.

Hurley had one high school, and their fans were rabid. They had a quarterback by the name Florian Helinski, who later had a big career at Indiana University. To put things in some context, Kenosha's Alan Ameche, a great Wisconsin running back who eventually won the Heisman Trophy in 1954, would play against Helinski for what would be the state title in Wisconsin.

PEOPLE, PLACES, AND THINGS

So I was standing on top of a bakery truck, doing Hurley versus Ironwood. It was a cold and rainy November night. All of a sudden, this gust of wind came along and blew every note on the information board into a snow bank.

These days, as I do high school games for a website named Vootage.com, it feels as if I've come full circle. Last season, I sat on scaffolding 60 feet high in the night air for a game at Crespi High in Encino, California. I keep thinking, "I've done this before." Talk about déjà vu.

I've experienced other crazy, embarrassing moments. Back in the '50s when I did Bradley basketball, we faced Memphis State at the 1957 NIT championship. Eddie Einhorn, the budding TV mogul who now owns the Chicago White Sox, came to WMBD in Peoria, where I was working at the time, and asked if I'd like to do the play-by-play for a small network of TV stations he had strung together in upper New York, Maine, New Hampshire, and Vermont. Einhorn took on the role of colorman.

We did the broadcast from the old Madison Square Garden on Eighth Avenue. The table they gave us to use was so small and narrow that you had to slide your legs under it and into the seat in order to sit down. Then you had to look down at the game. Einhorn told me that Red Auerbach, who was scouting the game—looking at players like Bobby Joe Mason and Dennis Butcher—for the Boston Celtics, was going to be our halftime guest.

When, Auerbach made his way to our spot, he was left standing between us. Much to our embarrassment, there was nowhere for him to sit.

When the camera came back on after a commercial, I said, "Hello again, welcome back to the Garden in New York City, I'm Tom Kelly, and for those of you just looking in, the gentleman to the far right is Eddie Einhorn," because people watching in Central Illinois didn't know who he was. "And you all know Red Auerbach, the famed coach of the Boston Celtics."

Tom Kelly, right, and Frank Gifford are courtside at Madison Square Garden before the 1966 NIT finals. *Photo courtesy of Tom Kelly*

Then Einhorn said, "Yes, and hello to all of you. I'm Eddie Einhorn and this is Tom Kelly," because he wanted to introduce me to the viewers in upstate New York and along the Eastern border.

Auerbach, cigar in hand, looked back and forth at both of us and finally said, "Are you two guys for real?" He was probably wondering how the heck he'd ever gotten involved in the conversation.

One year, CBS hired me to do an NIT finals telecast in New York. Hal Uplinger was the producer, and Tony Verna, who would later do the first instant replay in a game on national TV, was the director. While we were watching one of the Thursday night preliminary games, Tom Posten, one of the funny actors of the time and a friend of Uplinger's, joined us at the old Garden. After the first game ended, fans recognized him as they walked by. One person finally asked him, "When do you do your TV show, *What's My Line?*"

Posten just gave the fan a blank stare. "Thursday nights," he said. "We do it at a studio 30 blocks away from here at eight o'clock."

It was 8:30 p.m. He panicked and ran to a phone to call the studio, but thankfully, they had already found a replacement.

In 1967, Southern Illinois and Walt Frazier played Marquette for the title. Frank McGuire, then the head coach at South Carolina, and Frank Gifford, who worked at the CBS affiliate in New York, were on the eighth floor in a makeshift studio complete with a chalkboard, where McGuire could do Xs and Os to demonstrate team plays. I was on the floor giving the network play-by-play. It was a great moment. Doing the game with Gifford, who I really admired from his days at USC, was a real feather in my cap.

Southern Illinois won. I was putting my notes together and tallying up my box score to tell the game's statistics on the air. Suddenly, a gentleman wearing a Chesterfield coat with satin lapels and holding a Borsalino hat walked up to me. He said he was from Marquette, perhaps a school administrator, and that he would like to talk on the air for a moment. I told him I couldn't make that decision, but would contact the producer and ask him. I called Uplinger and told him about the gentleman, and he said he'd come down.

Uplinger met the man and told him to stay put. To me, he said, "Do the wrap-up and say goodbye." I did so, collected my notes, packed my bag, and left the arena to visit my sister in New Jersey. To this day, I believe that gentleman is still standing there, waiting to make his appearance on TV.

I forgot to mention one other crazy place I've covered a game. In 1998, Craig Fertig and I were doing the USC-Florida State game in Tallahassee, Florida. UCLA had already canceled its game against

Miami that weekend because of a hurricane threat. The rain was coming down as we were preparing to do the broadcast in the press box. Some people in our crew were avoiding me and whispering to one another as if they didn't want to tell me something. Finally, someone spoke to Fertig, who said, "I'm not going to tell him, you tell him."

"Tell me what?" I asked.

"Well, they don't have any room in the press box for you," someone said.

"So where will we do the broadcast?"

"See that building down at the end of the field? There's a table down there, and you'll have access to a restroom."

Well, Fertig and I did the game from there. I don't know if anyone has ever had to broadcast a football game looking at the field from that angle, but you cannot tell what yard line the players are on.

The payoff came when we were having a pregame meal in the press box. The PR director of Florida State came up to me and said, "Mr. Kelly, I just want to tell you how wonderful it is that you're here and how proud we are to have you."

"Thank you very much," I said.

And, as he was walked away, I said to Fertig, "Where would they have put us if they hated us?"

A LEGITIMATE CONCERN

In addition to doing play-by-play for the San Diego Chargers, I was also given the chance to broadcast some Oakland Raiders exhibition games while working at KTTV Channel 11.

I can recall one Saturday contest when the Raiders faced the Chicago Bears in the Midwest. Chicago was leading 50-0, and the Raiders decided very late in the game to try a field goal, a 50-yarder by the great George Blanda. The snap came back and rolled away from the holder. Blanda, a quarterback instinctively picked it up and looked downfield. He threw a pass to big Ben Davidson, a defensive standout who happened to be on special teams. The ball hit Davidson right between the two 8s on his jersey. He had the most astonished look on his face. I can't recall anyone ever throwing a pass to him before.

I said the pass was incomplete. Just then, the public address announcer came on and said, "Flag on the play . . . illegitimate receiver downfield." I took that moment to pause, then continued, "I don't know, but I think the term 'illegal' would be the proper term. I can't quite call a man as big as Ben Davidson 'illegitimate.'"

That Monday, I was working at KNX Radio when the phone rang. It was a woman calling from Pasadena.

"Mr. Kelly?"

"Yes."

"My name is Mrs. Davidson. I'm Ben's mother."

"Yes, what can I do for you?"

"I just called to thank you for pointing out that, when Ben was born, his father and I were married."

ANN MEYERS DRYSDALE
ENSHRINED IN THE NAISMITH BASKETBALL HALL OF FAME: 1993

One of the greatest athletes of all time didn't go to USC.

Ann Meyers married Don Drysdale. Her brother was a great basketball player at UCLA, and she's now the general manager of the WNBA's Phoenix Mercury.

Every year, Ann sends me a Christmas card of her three children. What a handsome family.

Ann couldn't make it when I was inducted into the Southern California Sports Broadcasters Hall of Fame, but she sent me a card that said, "Just for me, wear something blue." So I did. I wore a blue suit with a blue striped tie for the occasion.

I broadcast several games with Ann for the WNBA on Fox. I even played a few rounds of golf with her. She has a home on SeaCliff

Country Club in Huntington Beach, and her backyard is right next to a tough uphill par-3.

She's a great friend.

BILLY BARNES
UCLA FOOTBALL COACH: 1958-1964

Billy Barnes, a major who served in the Pacific in World War II, was a top aide to Red Sanders (1949-1957) at UCLA. He was also the Bruins coach who almost spoiled USC's 1962 season with a late 3-0 lead before Beathard, Brown, and Ben Wilson won the game 14-3 en route to the national title.

Billy was once a three-year starter at Tennessee for General Bob Neyland. We see each other often at Riviera, and he's always good for a smile and a happy memory. We'll always be linked: a couple of years ago, the American Football Coaches honored Billy the same night I was given the Lindsay Nelson broadcasting award.

BACK TO HIGH SCHOOL

When people ask me what I'm doing these days and I tell them I do a number of high school football and basketball games on the Internet, they often give me a strange look.

The Internet?

I have had trouble adjusting to the 21st century. If you were to give me a computer, it would take me from now until next Saturday to figure out how to turn the damn thing on. My daughter, Kathy, takes care of all that. But lately, I've been doing play-by-play for some magnificent contests involving many of today's great high school talent for Vootage.com, a new website that carries games beyond the United States and, as they tell me on the production truck, to China and Japan and Russia and Europe. Think about that. There will never be another world war as we've known it. This entire globe is so tied up together that it can't happen. Everyone is now holding hands economically, to say nothing of spiritually or philosophically. We're all in this together.

The Vootage approach, which was started by Jeff Proctor and his company, is as simple as clicking on a game and looking up statistics for players and quarters. How far have we come? Too far? I don't know, but Vootage is great.

The players and games we've done have me looking forward to the time when I'll see Orange Lutheran's Aaron Corp, Oaks Christian's Casey Clausen, or Canyon Country's J.J. Di Luigi play in college. You can just sit back on a Saturday afternoon and flip the dial to witness some outstanding talent. These kids are tremendous.

No one's carrying me to the press box and it's not plush these days, but frankly, I'm happy to still be doing games. And so far, no one's complained.

The fact that people still know me makes me feel really good. It's great when someone hears my voice, looks at me, and finally asks, "Are you Tom Kelly?" I don't know of anyone, unless he's is in a police lineup, who doesn't love to be recognized. Someone will remember a game I did 20 years ago. And if he remembers it, I remember it.

When a person takes the time to come up and talk to me, it makes me feel good. And, thanks to USC, I still go to every home game. I go down to the field and then up to the press box, seeing everyone from Sam Cunningham to Aaron Emanuel to Chris Hale and others too numerous to mention. I still count my blessings.

I now climb up into press boxes with escape ladders and no facilities if nature calls. But so far, we've managed to make it all right.

11

LONGTIME FANS

THE TROJANS FAN WEBSITE, WeAreSC.com, asked readers to contribute their favorite Tom Kelly stories. Here are some of them:

CHRIS RAINES
RESIDENT OF SAN JOSE, CALIFORNIA

In 1972, my family moved from Orange, California, to Honolulu, Hawaii—not a bad place for a 13-year-old boy. I was, up to that point in my life, a diehard Dodgers and USC Trojans fan. I loved them both equally and one never interfered with the other. Moving to Hawaii really concerned me, though; I was scared to death that I would never hear Dodgers or Trojans games on the radio or see them on TV as much. Could you imagine having to go without Vin Scully and Tom Kelly waxing eloquently over the radio as they delivered every last detail of every single game? I couldn't.

But after we moved, I found out we were in luck. The Hawaiian Gods loved Dodgers baseball and Trojans football. A contract amongst the powers that be in the island radio business allowed the Dodgers to broadcast games every weekend. As far as Trojans football went, I wasn't quite as lucky, though we did get the big games over the radio (and on TV, but not until a week later!). When one came on, it was like old times—Tom Kelly, whose voice was Trojans football, called the game and made it feel like a Saturday afternoon in the fall amidst cardinal and gold. It brought a kid back home to his roots for four hours.

Of course, the game I recall the most was the 1974 USC-Notre Dame match-up. My dad, brother, and I were outside building a brick patio in our backyard. I turned on the radio, knowing the big game was on. At the end of the first half, I was a mess and not happy at all. Laying bricks was the best way to release my frustration. But then the second half began. I can still hear Tom Kelly calling Anthony Davis' run back, Pat Haden's touchdown passes, and the stifling defense that shut Notre Dame down.

From a little kid who has grown up, I say thank you to Tom Kelly for doing his job so well and making it so fun for the rest of us. And, by the way, my dogs got out of quarantine and went on to live 10-plus years in the islands!

CHIP AVERY
RESIDENT OF CALABASAS, CALIFORNIA

As a third-generation Trojan, I have never known anything but USC football. My parents first bought season tickets in 1968 when I was seven. As a child, I usually got to attend one game a year, but more often than not, I sat at home and listened to the game on the radio. As a result, Tom Kelly's voice will forever be imprinted on my mind.

Several years ago, I was in my seats at a Dodgers game when I heard his voice. I honestly felt a chill as my childhood came back to me. I turned around and there he was, sitting right behind me. I was not surprised to find that he was as kind in person as I expected he would be.

CLAYTON DE LEON
RESIDENT OF LOS ANGELES, CALIFORNIA

My favorite Tom Kelly game is the USC-Notre Dame contest he "called" that made it on the big screen in *The Godfather, Part II*. That immortalized the great game for the general public. It is a microcosm of what it means to be American.

In my vast collection of USC Trojans memorabilia, I also have several LP recordings. My favorite is *Highlights of USC's 1964 Football Season*, edited from Tom Kelly's KNX/CBS broadcasts.

Thank you for being Mr. USC.

MICHAEL STAGG
RESIDENT OF ATHENS, GEORGIA

Tom Kelly was as much a part of my sports consciousness as a kid growing up in L.A. as Vin Scully and Chick Hearn.

My favorite Tom Kelly memory was listening to the 1990 USC-Cal game on the radio. USC's kicker, Quin Rodriguez, was not exactly having a stellar year. He had been having consistency problems. At the end of the game, USC got just within field-goal range on third down. So Rodriguez came on, lined up, and kicked.

Kelly said, "The kick is up. It looks long enough. . . . I don't believe it; he made it."

Even an *L.A. Times* writer commented on Tom's call the next day.

Tom Kelly was the consummate pro. He had a wonderful voice and he adored USC. What's not to love?

DARRELL E. WAGONER
RESIDENT OF SANTA BARBARA, CALIFORNIA

As a longtime Trojans fan (circa 1962), I feel that Tom Kelly deserves the same status as a coach or player. One could not imagine Trojans football without Tom Kelly. He was as closely associated with USC football as Chick Hearn was with the Lakers or Vin Scully was with the Dodgers.

My favorite memory is hearing Tom say, "Well, it's been an Irish afternoon," in that 1974 USC-Notre Dame game. The start of the second half began with those words. "It's a boy!" has to be second.

12

KELLY'S COLLEAGUES SPEAK UP

FROM THE DOZENS OF BROADCAST PARTNERS, behind-the-scenes colleagues, and even a loving daughter come the following stories about Tom Kelly and his work over the years:

MIKE GARRETT
USC ATHLETIC DIRECTOR
TV BROADCAST PARTNER

I remember coming to USC as a freshman in 1962. This big rally was being held next to Tommy Trojan. I didn't know of Tom Kelly then, but I heard this voice—a voice that was bigger than life—talking to Pete Beathard, Hal Bedsole, Willie Brown, and Damon Bame. He was introducing the team that had just won the national championship to the student body. He set the tone for the McKay years and those subsequent to that for me.

I always considered Tom Kelly to be part of the team and an important element of the dominant program. And later, as I got to know him, I realized what a fine announcer he was—one of the best in the business.

I was listening to the tapes of some games from the '60s as we were preparing to put them on our website, and hearing Tom's radio broadcasts reminded me of how he had created the USC aura. As big as John McKay and everything else were, Kelly put all the pieces together and made them accessible to everyone. As Chick Hearn was to the Lakers and Vin Scully is to the Dodgers, Tom's been our Hall of Famer, on par with them.

In the five years we worked together on football TV broadcasts, I didn't talk very much. It's true, Tom loves to talk and he had this continuous conversation with the listeners. But I always enjoyed hearing him speak as well, so I didn't mind watching the game as he announced. I never felt drowned out. I knew how good he was, so it didn't take any effort.

Tom was also very good at recalling facts. Trojans fans still come up to him and ask him questions, and his memory is unbelievable. He's a perfectionist. I love just listening to him talk. Even now, when I play golf with him, he'll say, "Hey No. 20, you remember when . . . ?" He still has those great pipes.

I like personalities such as his—those that are bigger than life. McKay was just the same. To me, he and the announcer go hand in hand.

When Tom talks to me about the program, I still listen—even today. Pete Arbogast now does the radio play-by-play for us. He's good, and I don't want to compare. But Tom will always be the standard for USC.

JOHN ROBINSON
FORMER USC HEAD FOOTBALL COACH
TV BROADCAST PARTNER

Tom Kelly wasn't just the announcer throughout the time I was at USC, but was there forever and seemed to be a part of everything. I always thought he was first and foremost a good guy. He was put in a difficult position, to talk about a program honestly and objectively. This becomes a little complicated. People always want to say what's wrong with what's going on in a game. If Tom was feeling the same way, that

KELLY'S COLLEAGUES SPEAK UP

was tough to balance. And yet he was so passionate. There were plenty of times that I was in the booth with him when he'd sound very matter-of-fact when the microphone was on, but when that mike went off during a break, he'd say, "Jeez, what's going on here? I can't believe it!" Then he'd go back on the air, completely professional.

When I was coaching, we'd have a Monday lunch with the media every week. Sometimes they'd get boring, so I was always looking for someone to save things—to ask something funny. I think Tom always sat back in the room, but when things got a little stale, I'd give him a look and he'd come up with some question to liven things up. He'd save me all the time.

He was always in awe when asked to be the MC at Trojans functions, but he was always enthusiastic and represented the school well. Sometimes people can go overboard, introducing politics and anger toward the other side. I always liked Tom—as someone important, he maintained a level of balance.

Even as a coach, I always saw him as one of us. There are many people around teams who want to be a part of things but really aren't. Tom was a part of our team. When we had good times, we wanted to include him.

I had a lot of fun being around him. His voice was so unique and commanding. You could still hear it a block away. And it's always good to have a voice connected to a program. Growing up, I'll always remember the voices connected to the teams I loved.

All those voices come and go as you grow older, but the guy who tells you what is going on every game—the good news and the bad news—becomes a part of your overall emotional attachment to a team.

Tom is one of the most distinctive voices in L.A. He's in the USC Hall of Fame and it's well deserved.

PAT McCLENEHAN
FORMER PRIME TICKET FEATURE/GAME PRODUCER
SENIOR VICE PRESIDENT/STATION MANAGER AT KCAL/KCBS IN LOS ANGELES

Tom Kelly and I go back 27 years, when I was just coming out of USC. I got a job as a stage manager for a sports odds show out of Las Vegas called *Las Vegas SportsView*, which Tom hosted with Jim Brown at the Stardust in front of a live audience on Monday nights.

I ended up directing that show and eventually had my own production company. Tom and I later formed McClenehan-Kelly Productions when we worked on a series called *Video Gold*, which took us around the country together as we interviewed more than 80 players and coaches about USC's football history.

Nobody cares more about USC football than Tom Kelly. He takes such pride in knowing all its players and its history. No one has seen it as he has, nor been more of a constant thread in it than he has. The best thing about traveling with him was listening to him interview all these people so enthusiastically. He was in heaven while doing that project.

Of course, the other best thing about the trip was that you always knew you were set up to play at the very best golf courses. If we were in Tulsa, we went to Southern Hills. If in New York, we played at Baltusrol. If in Pennsylvania, Oakmont. In Washington, Sahalee. In Denver, Cherry Hills. This tradition continued when I produced USC games. Every trip to Notre Dame we made time to play a round or two.

While working together at Prime Ticket, Prime Sports, and the USC magazine show, I always referred to him as "One-Take Tom." He was such a consummate professional. When you gave him five bullet points to work into a show's opening and told him he had 45 seconds to deliver them without a script, he'd deliver all five right on time. And he'd always do it on the first take. It was uncanny. But in our business, we do a second take just in case the first one didn't record properly. It used to drive Tom up the wall. "What was wrong with that one?" he'd

KELLY'S COLLEAGUES SPEAK UP

ask. "What do you mean?" He never got the concept, so it became a running gag. He was such a pro when he did voiceover work. He'd read a 30-second commercial in 28 and a half seconds, which is about right. If we needed a little more padding, we'd ask him to do it in just 28 seconds. So he'd read the same copy, taking a half second off.

There will never be another Tom Kelly. He's a true craftsman at a time when many athletes are moving into the booth after their careers end. He could have been a voice at a national network—he had that kind of talent and those kinds of pipes. Even today, he's very gifted. His voice sounds exactly the same.

JEFF PROCTOR
LONGTIME SOUTHERN CALIFORNIA TV SPORTS PRODUCER
CO-CREATOR OF VOOTAGE.COM

Tom was really encouraging to me when I first started out in television and aspired to become the next Tom Kelly. Despite having no training whatsoever, my dream was to become a play-by-play announcer. Tom encouraged me and put in a good word when Prime Ticket decided to eliminate some key positions from their college baseball coverage during a budget cut. As a production assistant with college baseball experience and a desire to work in front of the camera, I was asked to be a baseball analyst on Prime Ticket. Although most MLB games have a minimum of six cameras and most college games have at least four, we only used two: one in centerfield and one behind home plate.

Tom was great with me, always telling me to prepare for every game and promising to put in a good word for me. I had the unbelievable opportunity to travel with Tom as his Pac-10 analyst for two years. I was a 24-year-old kid who didn't know the first thing about makeup or hairspray or how else I needed to prepare for being on camera. That's where Tom came in.

Tom and I had to do our opening stand-up from the roof of the press box at Washington State. The wind was blowing pretty hard and my hair was flying all over the place. Tom looked at me, shook his head, and reached into his briefcase, where he kept everything a professional needed. He pulled out a can of hairspray, muttered a couple of expletives, and sprayed the top of my head. I don't know if his encouraging words and promises of recommendations were real or not, but I do know that as I took to the air with a hairsprayed mohawk on the roof of the Washington State press box that day, I determined working behind the scenes would be a much safer course of action.

Although Tom is one of the smartest guys I've ever worked with, he does not suffer fools and is quite stubborn. As a producer, I would frequently try to feed information to Tom during the course of a game, saying something to the effect of, "Hey Tom, so-and-so has 15 points and 12 rebounds." Invariably, some situation or another in the truck had kept me from hearing Tom announce those exact facts only moments earlier. At that point, Tom would throw one of these bon mots, as he calls them, into his commentary: "Ladies and gentlemen, so-and-so has 15 points and 12 rebounds, but you already know that since I mentioned it only moments ago. My producer would like me to mention it again, apparently, as he didn't hear me say it." Afterward, I made sure to listen to every word he said.

As an executive producer, I frequently asked Tom to do play-by-play for a number of different projects. He could literally do anything and has probably done most of the world's top sporting events. I once asked Tom to do a high school football game that, quite frankly, was beneath him at the time. But hearing Tom's voice do that game gave it more of a big-time feel. Imagine how cool it was for a high school kid to hear the Voice of the Trojans calling his name during a televised regular-season game. Tom wasn't pleased that he had to do the game, but after a bit of yammering at me, he gave his usual great call.

During halftime, Tom was reading off first-half stats when the lights went out in the press box. Oftentimes, high school accommodations appear a bit lacking when compared to the relatively luxurious L.A. Memorial Coliseum press box, and this was no different. But no one at home knew that the electricity had gone out because Tom made it through the stats perfectly to commercial break. Only then, when he knew he was safe, did he turn to the stage manager and say, "I'm going punch Jeff Proctor in the nose for putting me here." I think that was the last time I got him to do a high-school game prior to Vootage.com. I'm happy to say that he loves the high school game now.

No question about it, Tom can be a curmudgeon, but no one is more loyal and more kindhearted. If you are his friend, he'll do anything for you. Underneath that gruff exterior is one of the greatest guys you'll ever know.

DR. BOB FRANCIS
USC GAME SPOTTER FOR KELLY FOR 33 YEARS
TEAM CARDIOLOGIST FOR 15 YEARS

With ABC's coverage on one side and the opponents' on the other, being in the booth was always a great seat. As a 1957 USC medical school alum and a close friend of Marv Goux's, I had been fortunate enough to start as a spotter for Mike Walden back on USC radio games in 1969. When Mike moved on to do more TV in 1971, Tom came back to radio and inherited me—we even had that 12-0 team in 1972.

The one thing I can always say about Tom Kelly is that he's honest. If the referees—or the zebras, as he called them—made a bad call, the tone of his voice would increase as he harped on it. And when the Trojans made a mistake, he wouldn't sugarcoat it like a lot of so-called homers. He spoke the truth and the facts.

The most excited I've ever seen him was in the second half of that 1974 USC-Notre Dame game. He really waxed eloquently. Years afterward, whenever Anthony Davis would come into our booth, Tom would say, "There's Sweetness himself!"

From left to right, Tom Kelly is joined at Julie's Restaurant with Dave Levy, Craig Fertig, and Dr. Bob Francis. *Photo courtesy of Tom Kelly*

The most difficult time we had communicating was in 1979 during a game at LSU. That was the loudest stadium I'd ever been in, surpassing even Notre Dame. The metal stadium just made everything so much louder. We were all shoulder to shoulder, and none of us could hear each other. Like Paul McDonald down on the field, we resorted to hand signals. USC still won that game 10-7.

I was always the one with a camera in the press box, so I snapped photos all the time. Tom might have given me a rough time about it at first, but the pictures of him always came back with a warm smile.

Tom demonstrated a better memory for sports facts and details than anyone I've known. He could charm an angry lion—a phrase he'd often use—and I've seen him do so in press boxes and on golf courses.

KELLY'S COLLEAGUES SPEAK UP

In all our travels together, we tried to play golf on either the Friday before or early Saturday morning prior to a game. We saw a number of wonderful courses near Purdue, Ohio State, Alabama, and Arkansas. His love for golf helped him prepare for the broadcast.

Many of our stories come from the golf course, where he's a stickler for the rules. He's the same way about life.

Once, we were playing golf in Tucson, Arizona, before USC's game at the University of Arizona. Two other friends were with us, and Tom was in a hurry to play from the start. Usually, the person farthest from the hole hits first, but Tom wanted to play "ready golf," meaning if you were ready, you hit it. So all day was like a march.

We got to one green, and I was about 60 feet away. Tom was in a trap and everyone else was below us. So I putted, and, as luck would have it, it rolled in. Tom bellowed from the trap, "Two-stroke penalty, no one was tending the cup!" I thought he didn't care. I was angry and it cost me money. But that was typical Tom.

Another time, he visited me at Hacienda. I was driving the cart and he was giving me directions the whole way. Everyone could hear us coming. On a dogleg right hole, we started down a hill. Halfway down, he said, "No! Turn!" So I turned left, and the forward momentum threw him out of the cart. He went down the hill, rolling over and over and screaming obscenities. The other guys we were with were laughing. Tom walked up to the back of the cart, took my clubs off, threw them on the ground, and got in the driver's seat, saying, "I'm never riding with you again." I had to beg just to get my clubs back.

Tom's been such a unique person; he's absolutely and unequivocally the Voice of the Trojans. He was a gentleman to me on and off the air, and an inspiration to work with.

JIM PERRY
USC SPORTS INFORMATION DIRECTOR: 1974-1984
RADIO BROADCAST PARTNER: 1977-1983

The first thing that impressed me about Tom Kelly was how comfortable he was behind a microphone. You'd think he could fall out of bed and call a game. He talked as if he'd rehearsed what he was saying for years. But he shared something rare with me before my first game in 1977. We were having lunch at Julie's, talking about how we'd make this broadcasting partnership work. I had been interviewed many times on radio, but I hadn't done color on a game. He said to me, "Don't worry. The live microphone can be intimidating, but just talk and relax and you'll be fine." Then, he added, "That mike can intimidate me sometimes." I'll never forget that. After thinking about it, I realized that wasn't something he'd normally tell anyone. Even if he was just saying it to try to make me feel comfortable, it showed that he even found it difficult sometimes, which was great for me to hear.

As I quickly learned, though, Tom Kelly wasn't shy about revealing his feelings. Sometimes before games, he was so keyed up and irritable that he intimidated people. I thought that our engineer, Tom Goodwin, was like Gary Burghoff's "Radar" character from *M*A*S*H*, whereas Kelly was like MacLean Stevenson's character, "Colonel Blake." Letting off steam, they barked at each other simultaneously and never listened to each other, but they knew what they were talking about. Then they went out and did a great game. I'm sure the people in the press box must have been wondering what they were yelling about all the time.

The only time I can remember Tom getting upset with me was during a game at Notre Dame. We came out of a commercial and listened to a few seconds of the Notre Dame fight song. When it finished, I said, "That's a catchy tune."

Tom looked at me and said, "Catchy tune? That's a famous fight song, and you call it a 'catchy tune'?"

KELLY'S COLLEAGUES SPEAK UP

He couldn't believe I had said that. Maybe it offended him.

Tom was often critical of the zebras, too. On the very first play of the Notre Dame game in 1977, the Irish had a 3-yard run. USC's defense stuffed it, but a flag fluttered out and USC was called for grabbing the facemask, a 15-yard penalty. Tom was already indignant. "Well if that's the kind of day it's going to be, the Trojans should go home right now," he said. And he was right. Notre Dame won 49-19 against a great John Robinson team. Some may say that Tom was just ranting, but his words were prophetic. And it was the only time Robinson lost to the Irish in his first run as coach.

Like any real fan, Tom was sometimes tough on USC, saying the Trojans were "their own worst enemy." That may have made him miss a few things.

In a game at Stanford in 1980—one that USC would win 34-9—the Cardinal had the ball near midfield, and quarterback John Elway was being chased by the entire USC line. Elway must have gone back 20 yards before he finally wheeled around, planted, and threw a line drive past Ronnie Lott that hit Ken Margerum on the goal line for a 46-yard touchdown. The ball must have traveled more than 60 yards. It was one of the most incredible plays I'd ever seen. My mouth was open and nothing came out. But Kelly's initial reaction was that USC had screwed up and shouldn't have allowed that play to happen. I finally said, "Tom, we've just seen one of the most amazing plays ever."

Tom wasn't one to throw out compliments, either, so I didn't always know where I stood with him. We went on the road in Washington a couple of years after I first began working with Tom. A friend of Tom's also made the trip. She and I were talking in a restaurant, and she said, "You know, he really likes you and he thinks you're doing a good job." He'd never tell me that, but the fact that she shared it with me was interesting.

Another time, Tom did startle me with a great gesture. I had a really good pair of binoculars that I used at home games, but they were too heavy to take along on the road, so I brought along this cheap plastic pair. One day, out of the blue, Tom gave me a brand new pair of binoculars, saying, "I thought you could use these." I was very touched. They were light and very good and I used them for a very long time.

After listening to and then working with Tom for so many years, I believe he's underrated. You have to remember that, many years ago, NCAA rules prohibited a team from appearing on TV more than four times a year, so if you weren't at the USC game, you had to listen to Tom Kelly's call. You depended on him, and he always had the basics down. He told you where the ball was, the distance of a pass play, who recovered the fumble—things you may now take for granted. He was conscious of every little detail. TV broadcasters don't always have such radio background now.

He has a great natural voice and was always very dramatic. If a game came down to the final seconds, he was really into it. He captured the excitement, something not everyone can do if they don't have the voice or the personality. He could see humor in many things, and always added that to the broadcast. And he was so smooth; you never felt he could be intimidated by anything. I think doing games came as naturally to him as brushing his teeth.

TIM TESSALONE
USC SPORTS INFORMATION DIRECTOR: 1984-PRESENT

For much of my tenure with the USC athletic department, Tom Kelly was the one constant. Players and coaches came and went, but for many years Tom Kelly was always there, as reliable as the morning sun.

USC people knew that Tom loved his Trojans, yet he never let that love interfere with any of his broadcasts. But non-Trojans had a difficult time listening to Tom because of that very affinity. They felt he was a "homer." While such criticism—which often appeared in the media—was pointed and bordered on cruel, I never sensed that it bothered Tom.

KELLY'S COLLEAGUES SPEAK UP

My first encounter with Tom was a real eye-opener, as it gave me a rather vivid glimpse of this loud Irishman (that's redundant, no?) who I would end up working with throughout my Trojans career. It actually occurred during the first week I was employed by USC. In August of 1979, I was hired as an assistant sports information director, serving under Jim Perry. Back then, the Pac-10 organized an annual "Skywriters Tour," in which media from throughout the conference would travel to each of the league schools, visit with the football team during the day, write a preview story about that team that afternoon, and let off some steam at a school-hosted dinner at night.

On this particular evening, USC and UCLA co-hosted a dinner at a restaurant in Marina del Rey. Nearly 100 local and conference media were there, along with head coaches John Robinson and Terry Donahue and various athletic department staffers. After dinner, I walked into the bar and found Robinson holding court with Kelly and my fellow assistant SID, Dennis Kirkpatrick. Or rather, Kelly was holding court with those two. What began as a relaxed, post-dinner tete-a-tete soon turned into (with the help of some libations) a very boisterous and heated argument amongst the trio. Soon, many of the media came over to observe Kelly screaming at Robinson, Robinson yelling back at him, and Kirkpatrick jumping in to shout his two cents' worth. Of course, none of their arguments were making much sense because the drinks were kicking into high gear. And I was sitting there thinking, "What have I gotten myself into?" There stood the head coach of the defending national champion Trojans, a revered figure, getting an earful from this livid broadcaster and punk assistant SID. And vice versa. Was this how we treated our icons?

It turned out that Kelly was just being Kelly, Robinson was just being Robinson, and Kirkpatrick was just being Kirkpatrick. But for a neophyte staffer like me, I couldn't believe anyone would challenge—and seemingly disrespect—the USC head football coach or longtime Trojans broadcaster.

From that day on, though, I came to understand Tom and learned to respect him for his play-calling ability. No broadcaster was better at giving the listener down and distance and constant score updates—little things that today's play-by-play guys so often overlook as they trip over their words and anecdotes. He had a breadth of sports knowledge, calling everything from football and basketball to billiards and boxing. He had plenty of glibness; preparation was not one of Tom's strengths, but you usually couldn't tell that he hadn't done much homework. And, yes, his Irish dander. I've seen him scream for no apparent reason at many a producer, engineer, and stripe-shirted zebra. Oh mercy nurse! I always wondered how he could be such a good golfer with that temper.

And Tom was a trooper, too. He called games while sick with a high fever and while battling laryngitis (thanks to Dr. Bob Francis for many of those soothing throat medications that allowed Tom to get through a broadcast). And, like the mailman, not even inclement weather kept him from his appointed task. One year, he was on his way to Eugene, Oregon, to announce a Trojans-Ducks basketball game when his connecting flight in San Francisco was fogged out several hours before tip-off. Somehow, he managed to find his way north and walked into the arena 10 minutes before the game, truly flustered. But he called the game as if nothing had happened, evidence of the true professional that he was.

It was very gratifying for me when Tom was inducted into the USC Athletic Hall of Fame in 2001, and even more so when he was similarly honored by his peers, the Southern California Sports Broadcasters Association, in 2006. Those honors were well deserved for one of the best in the business.

KELLY'S COLLEAGUES SPEAK UP

MARK WALTON
FOX SPORTS NET PRODUCER/CAMERAMAN

TK and I first worked together on the history of USC football way back in the mid-'80s. I did camerawork and lighting on many of the interviews for those programs, so I was able to see Tom's people skills firsthand. The man had a gift. Whenever someone sat down for an interview, whether it be Mike Garrett, Marcus Allen, or someone not nearly as famous, TK immediately made him feel like he was the most important person on the planet and that his contributions to the great Trojans football heritage were as important as anyone else's.

I have never known anybody in my life with a better command of the English language. I will always remember that his favorite things to do during downtime were crossword puzzles. They were a passion of his and, considering his incredibly strong vocabulary, obviously paid off. I think he was practically born with this skill, but the crossword puzzles just added more depth.

We worked together for many years on the *USC Sports Magazine* show. Tom had the amazing ability to do his stand-ups in just minutes. He was so gifted with language that he could literally construct what he was going to say within seconds of being told the subject matter. Then he would stand in front of that camera and perform it perfectly. This is an ability I'm not sure many will appreciate, but please believe me when I say that TK was by far the quickest, sharpest, and most talented person I have ever worked with.

Tom and I probably experienced our best times together working on our show, *Golf the West*. It was a great opportunity for both of us to do that show because we both love the game and understand how important the great variety of courses is to most golfers. We were both a little shocked when it was taken off the air. One of our most memorable shows may have been the one in which PGA Tour professional Fred Couples took us on a tour of a beautiful course in Simi Valley called Lost Canyons. To get Fred, the one stipulation was that we had to shoot the entire thing in about an hour and a half. Kyle Reischling and I started praying immediately because it usually took an entire day to shoot one of those shows. Lo and behold, Fred and TK were able to take us on their tour in less than 90 minutes.

This could only have happened with Tom leading the way. He had such a remarkable ability to be spontaneous and make sense at the same time. On that particular day, Tom didn't have any time to think through what he was going to say to Fred. Yet, it turned out to be one of the best shows we ever did, and for obvious reasons: a beautiful and extremely visual golf course was being shown off by one of the nicest and most genuine Tour pros I have ever met and quite possibly one of the best golf show hosts of all time.

GREG TAYLOR
FOX SPORTS NET DIRECTOR OF CREATIVE SERVICES

My first assignment as a show producer was working with Tom on *This Week in Southern California Sports.* We shot most of Tom's package lead-ins in the studio with the script on the Tele-Prompter, but took the show out of the studio for the first time when California Speedway was about to open in Fontana. I wrote the scripts for Tom's wraparounds. He took a look at the copy and then nailed it in the first take. Unaware that he was known as "One-Take Tom," I said after the read, "Nice job, Tom."

Mr. Kelly looked at me and said, "What were you expecting, a shank?"

I also worked with Tom on a boondoggle show in Australia. We were there to televise an Australian Rules football game matching former NFL players against former Australian Rugby League players. It wasn't much of a contest since neither team had any experience playing the game, but it was a great trip. The Australian Tourism Bureau asked us to cover the players as they went sightseeing through Sydney and the Outback. They organized a trip for some of us to check out an actual

KELLY'S COLLEAGUES SPEAK UP

Australian Rules football game, and we were a little surprised when Tom joined us on the bus. He had wanted to play golf in Sydney, but his cab driver couldn't find the course. Tom told all of us the story, and that the driver repeatedly apologized for being unable to find the course. Tom said that he told the cabbie, "Don't confuse me with someone who has the patience of Gandhi . . . I am a pissed off Irishman!"

Tom's loss was our gain. To have him at the game with us was a blast. He couldn't help but slip a little play-by-play in for the benefit of those sitting near him—and with his voice, that meant several rows of people. Tom also enjoyed the chant the locals were shouting for their team, the Bulldogs: "Doggy, Doggy, Doggy . . . Woof, Woof, Woof!"

Working with Tom was a blast. I found out that his bark was worse than his bite. The crew in the studio loved when he came in. One of my favorite memories with him will always be the time we taped the holiday edition of *This Week in So Cal* in the studio. My brother and a couple of his buddies, who Tom called "Santa and his Swinging Elves," added musical accompaniment. In between takes, the band was playing Tom was snapping his fingers and swinging around in the background, like the Frank Sinatra of Sports Broadcasters.

JIM WATSON
FOX SPORTS NET WEST/PRIME TICKET BROADCASTER

In November of 1977, I gave up two tickets to the USC-UCLA game to go skiing in Mammoth. I had just received my driver's license and a '71 sky blue Volkswagen van. Tropical curtains, a Coleman refrigerator, and a cassette player cranking the Doobie Brothers took a trip all the way up Highway 395.

SC had fallen out of the national championship picture and was only playing for a chance to knock UCLA out of the Rose Bowl. I figure it wasn't worth missing all that fresh powder and a chance to sit behind the wheel for the long drive.

I tried to put the game out of my mind, but by the time we had reached Lone Pine, I couldn't resist any longer. I popped out the cassette and started rolling the AM dial. Talk shows, news, mariachi music, preachers—wait, go back! Through the speakers' crackling interference came that booming voice like a foghorn in the night: "A hearty good evening to you and yours on a brisk night from the Coliseum."

I was lucky. I grew up in Southern California when the local roster of sportscasters included Vin Scully, Dick Enberg, Al Michaels, and the Illinois baritone, Tom Kelly.

TK was synonymous with Trojans football. When you heard his voice, you knew it. It held court over a packed Coliseum with diamond designs in its end zones. Cardinal and gold stood at one end, powder blue and gold at the other.

We continued our drive toward the slopes, Kelly's narration prohibiting any conversation inside the car. The teams slugged it out and UCLA led 27-26 with just two minutes on the clock.

And then . . . nothing.

The radio cut out. The signal had been wavering for the past 20 miles, but now it was gone completely. My friend began frantically beating the dashboard as I jammed on the brakes and reversed our course. Back we raced into the Mojave Desert in search of an invisible beam of sound from the Coliseum press box.

A mile. Two miles. Five miles. Still nothing. Ten miles back, we finally picked up a faint signal. I yanked the van to the side of the road. Just two seconds remained on the clock and SC was deep in Bruins' territory. "Here comes Frank Jordan onto the field with a wink at destiny and a chance to win the game," Kelly said.

We couldn't stand it. We jumped out, opened up the sliding door, and stood there waiting on Kelly's call, which he delivered with his customary polish and panache.

"The snap, the hold, Jordan's kick is up . . . it's . . . GOOD! TROJANS WIN!"

KELLY'S COLLEAGUES SPEAK UP

UCLA was out of the Rose Bowl, Frank Jordan was cemented into the game's lore, and two dorks were jumping up and down on a deserted highway in the desert as if they were sitting on the 50-yard line.

Thirteen years later, I was hired by Fox Sports West to call games. On my first day there, I was introduced to Tom Kelly.

I held a nervous hand out in front of me and stammered, "Tom, I've been listening to you for years. It's a great honor to finally meet you in person."

Kelly looked me up and down and, with disdain dripping from his voice, uttered the words I can still hear today, "Damn right, it's an honor."

Then he walked away laughing.

I loved it.

JOHN PAPADAKIS
USC LINEBACKER: 1970-1971
 MOST INSPIRATIONAL PLAYER (1971)
CO-AUTHOR OF *TURNING OF THE TIDE*, THE BOOK ON THE 1970 USC-ALABAMA GAME
OWNER OF PAPADAKIS TAVERNA IN SAN PEDRO

If you think of the old *Untouchables* show with Elliott Ness, Tom Kelly's voice was similar to that of Walter Winchell, the ongoing commentator. Kelly's "Untouchables" were John McKay and his "Rat Pack" of coaches: Marv Goux, Dave Levy, Craig Fertig, and Willie Brown, all of whom helped him realize his coaching dream. Goux was the spiritual leader, Levy was the tactician, Fertig was the friendly tie to the youth, and Brown was the communicator of African-American values. No one could have interpreted that situation and how it all played out better than Tom Kelly. He understood because he was able to eat and drink with them. He was their broadcaster and their communicator.

Try to understand the era of the 1960s and '70s. Only a few sports journalists covered teams for newspaper, radio, and TV. They all commiserated with the coaches, and many were simply owned by them. The coaches handled the media. Every word that came out of the university had the stamp of the head coach, who had complete authority. One of the many things the coach had control over was his own image. The loyalty that McKay showed his assistants he also showed to Kelly.

Looking at ancient history, we had Homer, the Greek master poet, who recorded the Trojan Wars. And then we had Tom Kelly. Were it not for this Irish poet, no one would know about modern-day Troy. Tom Kelly was Homeric in his reciting of Trojans legends. And Tom is the romantic type, so his inclinations spilled out into his announcing. He applied all his fever and passion to the Trojans.

USC has its legendary stories just as Notre Dame has its legendary stories. Remember "Win one for the Gripper"? We all saw the movie. Did it actually happen? Who knows? Has it helped Notre Dame recruit and win? Yes, because the game of football isn't played in reality, it's played in the minds and the imaginations of young men. Football becomes a reality for them from their core. People play football for glory and recognition and the reward of confidence. Myths create the game and the legends.

Through the years, Tom Kelly was a great interpreter of the epic of USC history—an oral poet. He follows in a long line of the game's rhapsodic singers, like Chris Schenkel, Lindsay Nelson, and Curt Gowdy. As the Voice of the Trojans, Kelly went beyond what the newspapermen were doing at that time. McKay could use his wit to protect himself, and Kelly could mold it and relay the story to the people. The famous one in 1967 detailing the time McKay didn't want to take the field at Notre Dame revealed the nuances of McKay's personality. In many ways, Kelly helped define McKay and the legend of USC.

KELLY'S COLLEAGUES SPEAK UP

RICH MAROTTA
USFL/BOXING BROADCAST PARTNER

If Tom Kelly thinks I was well prepared, it might be because I was well prepared for him.

In 1964, when I was 14 years old, USC had a terrific football season, capped off by the 20-17 win over undefeated and top-ranked ranked Notre Dame. Shortly afterward, a USC football record album featuring Tom's radio calls of the year's many highlights was released. One side contained all the games prior to the Notre Dame upset; the other side was the entire amazing win over the Irish. I thought it was the greatest thing I'd ever heard. I wore that record out. It was actually the beginning of my sportscasting career, because I memorized the plays of the Notre Dame game and recited them, word for word, right along with Kelly. I'm sure I probably used many of those same phrases later on in my career. One line I still remember came after USC missed a touchdown pass. Kelly moaned, "It would've nullified all this nonsense!" Although it was 43 years ago, that sticks with me to this day. When I mentioned to Tom that I played this album over and over, he said in typically humble Kelly fashion, "Oh, you liked that one, huh, kid?"

I've had the good fortune to work with Tom in both football and boxing. While his technique of calling a game is breezy and somewhat blustery, he definitely enters every game or fight prepared to the tiniest detail. As a partner in the booth, if you want to keep up with him, you'd better be, too. Then there's that voice, always that voice. Unmistakable and unique, it's the greatest sportscasting voice ever.

Tom is so confident in his radio and TV play-by-play calls that he might come off as egotistical to some listeners or intimidating to some partners in the booth. However, I'll never forget what he told me before the first game we ever worked: "Just let me call the play, then I'll get out of your way. You say whatever you want and go as long as you want." What color man could ask for more?

When we did the KCAL fights for Forum Boxing, we often went on the road to Vegas or Tahoe. The day before, we had our fighter meetings, which were always a highlight. We rented some room where the six broadcasters (both English and Spanish-speaking) met the fighters to interview them and get notes for the following night's telecast. Tom was the king in his lair. One by one, the fighters came in to be greeted by Kelly's booming voice: "Come on in here, Marco Antonio, how ya doin'? Sit over there; the boys want to ask you some questions. . . . Don't bother with Marotta, though. He said you looked bad in that last fight."

Thanks a lot, Kelly.

Then there were the hilarious production meetings. Poor Susan Stratton, our producer, tried to conduct an orderly meeting a half-hour in length. It was totally futile. Tom's running commentary was so funny that we would all be on the floor laughing, and the meetings would stretch to an hour and a half. Susan, God bless her, would trudge on valiantly, giving us enough information so that not only would we do great telecasts, but we would win two local Emmys for them as well.

KATHY KELLY-BORISOFF
TOM KELLY'S DAUGHTER

My earliest memories of my father as a "sports announcer" relate specifically to the times I went to work with Dad.

I used to think that my father was the tallest man in the world. He has always been my hero and, in many ways, still seems larger than life to me.

When I was seven or eight, I remember going with my mom to pick up my dad at the airport in Peoria, Illinois. At that time, he announced

Former heavyweight boxing champion Joe Louis, left, poses with Tom Kelly, center, and KNX's George Martin at Lafayette Park in Los Angeles in the 1960s.
Photo courtesy of Tom Kelly

began to walk into the airport from the field, I kept looking for the tallest man—my dad, of course. The players kept coming and coming, and, near at the end of the line, I noticed this little guy. At 6-foot-1, he really wasn't little, but he sure was shorter than the others. As I looked closer, that little guy was my dad. It took me a while to adjust to that.

The first time I remember going to work with my dad was in Peoria. My birthday is in February, right in the middle of basketball season, and my dad was usually traveling. He always wished me a happy birthday over the radio, which was nice. But this particular year, the team had a home game and I got to go. I might have been six. I remember getting dressed up and sitting next to my dad at the announcer's table. In basketball, the announcers and spotters sit right on the playing floor, so I was pretty intimidated by all the action happening right in front of me. I kept asking my dad, "What's the score?" He didn't answer because he was busy giving the play-by-play. That didn't deter me. I thought he didn't hear me, so I kept asking. I pulled his jacket sleeve, leaned over, and looked him right in the eye—he didn't react in the slightest. The man spotting for Dad finally saved us all from going nuts by leaning over and telling me my dad couldn't answer because he was busy working. I finally got the message. I just knew I was in for a scolding—or at the least the dreaded stink eye—but my dad never mentioned it. It was, however, a long time before I got to go again.

Aside from his superior broadcasting skills, phenomenal memory, quick and sometimes sharp wit, the sound of his voice is what makes him memorable. I'm sure everyone has the sound of their parents' voices deeply embedded in their psyche. I feel this genetic ping whenever I hear my dad's voice. No matter where I am or what I'm doing, if I hear him say my name—even on voicemail messages—I'm alerted.

Listening to my dad's voice on the air is odd to me. It's the voice I've known forever and I recognize immediately. Yet, I know when others hear him, they think, "Oh, yeah, here's the game." I can tell whether he's happy, sick, really up, edgy because of a technical difficulty, or just irritated at a bad call. Hearing my dad's voice resonating from the surrounding transistor radios as I sat in the stands at USC football games was always a source of pride.

Once, a blind friend of mine told me that he loved to listen to Trojans football because the play-by-play announcer described the action so well that he could "visualize" the movement of the players. My friend didn't know that the announcer was my dad. I was very proud.

I remember two times when I was simply overwhelmed with emotion at hearing my dad's voice. The first was when I had been living in Colorado and hadn't talked to him in quite a while. I was driving from Denver to Fort Collins and turned on the radio for some music when some quirk of the weather and the effect of the Rocky Mountains on the radio waves brought in a Los Angeles Lakers basketball game—my dad was announcing. I was stunned and simply had to pull over just to hear the sound of his voice.

The second time was pretty funny. Dad gave my late husband and me tickets to a USC home game. My husband had never seen a football game before at the Coliseum, so it was quite an event. The seats were about 25 rows down from the press box. We were in our seats before the game as the Trojans Marching Band came on the field, looking quite impressive in their cardinal and gold uniforms. My husband was shocked and said in a really loud voice, "My God, they're pagans." Well, here we were in the middle of all these Trojans fans. I was embarrassed, because many of the fans had season tickets and knew that I was sitting in Tom Kelly's seats. I was staring at the field and hoping that the moment would pass when I heard the Voice calling my name. My head whipped around so fast; I thought that dad had heard my husband's "pagan" remark. When reality set back in, I saw Dad leaning out of the press box window, calling my name to give me a program. I was laughing and almost crying at the same time. Dad dropped the program down to a gentleman under the press box in the first row, and a person in each row passed it over to me. To this day, I don't know how I heard Dad's voice over the band and crowd noise.

Most folks wouldn't know that my dad has a soft spot for single mothers, young men and women in the armed forces, and boxers. He lobbied hard for several years to try to create a health, welfare, and pension fund for retired boxers and those hurt in the ring.

His memory is really uncanny. He can remember details of games that happened 40 years ago and repeat statistics from memory that most folks have to look up to verify. When we walk around and mingle at USC events and before football games, I'm amazed at how many former players he knows. Most fans don't get to see college football players' faces very often, especially if those players doesn't go into the pros. But Dad remembers.

Do you get the idea that I'm his biggest fan? I'll leave you with a story about his humble side, as hard as that might be to imagine.

I can't tell you how many times I've been with him when someone will hear him talking, recognize his voice, walk over, and introduce himself. At football games, their kids are usually with them and they want a picture taken with my dad. He is always touched by this and grateful that they think enough of him to ask. If people tell him that they really liked a certain event that he broadcast, he gets this little smile on his face and says something like, "Well, thank you very much." Then, depending on whether they're talking about golf, football, basketball, or boxing, Dad turns the conversation to them with questions about their interest in the sport and if their kids are involved. I don't know if he notices it, but I have, and I think it's kind of sweet.

13

AS USUAL, KELLY GETS THE LAST WORD

OVER THE YEARS, some listeners have called me a USC homer. Fine. Maybe I was.

But in Los Angeles' large market of broadcasters, which included Vin Scully, Chick Hearn, and Dick Enberg, I doubt I was the only one.

SPECULATION

After spending 40-some years covering one school, you have no idea how significant you are until you walk into the press box at a place like South Bend and other broadcasters want to know all about your team. It really gives you a sense of worth.

Maybe this influenced the fact that I was partial to the Trojans. I had a relationship with the players and the university. Over the years, USC has become a national entity. I don't care if you're on the playing field or in law, business, or medical school. Thousands of students from all over the world have represented this university, and I held a position of national prominence as their voice. It was very overwhelming and made me feel as if I belonged.

Or maybe I wasn't ready to step in and be objective. I came to USC from Illinois, which wasn't winning any Big Ten titles, and all of a sudden I was announcing national championship games. John McKay and his teams competed in the Rose Bowl against Wisconsin. Was I supposed to concentrate on being unbiased? I got all wrapped up in the excitement. Whether that's an excuse or a legitimate reason, I have no idea.

"OH MERCY NURSE!"

I do know that many people formed misguided opinions of me. Maybe this started with Jim Healy, who had a show on KABC opposite mine on KNX for many years. One day, Bob Crane, who I worked with at KNX, asked me if I had heard the things Healy was saying about me on the air. I honestly had never heard of Healy. I told Crane to let Healy know that if he really had a problem with how I called USC games, I'd arrange to have a broadcast credential for him at the next contest, and he could come up to the booth and do the first two quarters. Then, if I felt he was better than I was, I'd gladly step aside. Crane couldn't believe I'd actually do it, but that was my offer.

The next week, Crane asked me how the game went Saturday. I told him Healy never showed up—but I didn't really expect him to. From then on, whenever Healy referred to me on his show, he'd call me "Hysterical Harry" and play a tape of me saying, "Oh mercy nurse!" on a broadcast I had done.

I had plenty of other "catchphrases" that would have been more fitting, I suppose. "He couldn't have caught that with a dip net," was one of them. "He's as tough as a two-dollar steak," was another. But "Oh mercy nurse" was the one Healy decided to play over and over on his show.

Eventually, Healy helped spread a story that I had supposedly yelled at officials to take UCLA star basketball player Kenny Fields off the court during a game against USC at the Sports Arena one afternoon. What really happened? Fields got the ball on a breakaway, drove down the court, turned his ankle, and fell under the basket. Nothing seemed to be happening as Ducky Drake, UCLA's great athletic trainer, ran out on the floor to attend to him.

"They're going to have to stop play here and call a timeout and get him off the court," I said on the broadcast. "They're going to have to call a timeout and charge it to UCLA."

Booker Turner, who is among the great Pac-10 referees and to this day a dear friend, was standing five feet away. He looked at me, said, "You're right," blew his whistle, and charged UCLA with a timeout.

Two days later, I got a call from a local scribe who said he had received a great deal of mail and phone calls from people who listened to the game and were upset that I had said someone should have dragged Fields off the floor.

"I didn't say that," I told him.

"Do you want to answer the people who questioned it?" he asked.

"Who did they call? You? You answer them. If they want to call me, they know where to find me at KNX."

The bottom line is that I never said, "Get him off the floor." But Healy took what I did say out of context and perpetuated it. I guess he felt it was worth commenting on.

LOOKING FOR ANSWERS

Maybe the fact that I never cultivated a great romance with the scribes in town has something to do with the public's perception of me, too. Bud Tucker and Bud Furillo, two of the best newspapermen around, became color commentators for me, but other broadcasters in the business would cultivate a writer to the point that, if he was having a down day, there was no grist for his mill. If that's how they wanted to do it, fine. I just never went that way, and I'm too old to change my ways now.

When I was doing San Diego Chargers games at the same time I was doing USC, I'd go down into the press box in San Diego and Jerry Magee, the great *San Diego Union* writer, would greet me with "Hi, Tom.

How'd we do yesterday?" Rick Smith, the Chargers' public relations man, would always say to me, "Trojans!" The inference was that I was partial, but they were good-natured about it.

I'll say this in my defense. When we did a history of USC football in *Trojan Video Gold* along with a history of USC vs. UCLA in *Crosstown*, we interviewed former UCLA quarterback Gary Beban in his office downtown. He couldn't believe we would bother to talk to him for a USC project.

I've never had a player from another team tell me that I ignored his efforts or wasn't appreciative of his or his team's talent. No matter what color the uniform, I recognized talent and achievement. If anyone out there feels I denigrated him in any way, I guess I owe him an apology. But hopefully I don't have to apologize too much.

At any rate, one of my prized possessions at home on the wall is John Wooden's Pyramid of Success, autographed by the great UCLA coach himself. It says, "To my friend Tom Kelly, whose allegiance to another university in this town I never could quite understand. God Bless, John Wooden."

Maybe that answers any questions.

FROM MY PERSPECTIVE

The Lord blessed me with a voice that isn't objectionable to listeners, is recognizable by many, and has the ability to stand before people. I hope I didn't alienate anyone down the line, but I loved doing what I did and loved broadcasting for the team I covered.

It has been an unbelievable career. I have mentioned it before, but there's no rhyme or reason how I managed to remain the Voice of the Trojans for more than 40 years except luck and good fortune. I think about great announcers who did all the due diligence and knew everything about their teams and players, but toiled in absolute anonymity. They were never close to a Heisman Trophy, much less on a first-name basis with seven people who have won the award, and they

Tom Kelly flashes the USC "Victory" sign after he is presented with a scroll from Los Angeles County Board Supervisor Mike Antonovich during a ceremony in downtown L.A. in May of 2007. Danuska Kelly, left, looks on.
Photo courtesy of Los Angeles County

never had the opportunity to go to a Rose Bowl as witness to some of the finest games in a great athletic tradition. I don't know how I qualified, but I'm thankful. I enjoyed every moment and realize I was one of the fortunate ones.

Starting in 1962, I spent 41 years with the Trojans as they won 323 games with 119 losses and 12 ties. I saw USC achieve 14 wins in 23 bowl games. I watched them accumulate a 10-5 record in 15 Rose Bowls. I did games for five Heisman winners and was conversant with two others. I experienced four national championships—six if you include the most recent ones. And I witnessed some of the greatest names in coaching history prevail.

ACKNOWLEDGMENTS

IT'S TIME TO THANK A NUMBER OF PEOPLE who shared nearly five decades with me in the booth. In football, it started with Bill Symes, who may not have understood everything I was talking about but played it off well.

Other color men I must thank are, in no particular order: Craig Fertig, who was on TV with me for 15 years, one of my dearest friends, and one of the greatest assets to the school; John Robinson; Mike Garrett, who brought wonderful insight; Paul McDonald; Bud Furillo, who was a great Trojan and may have run the best sports section ever in this city at the *Herald Examiner*; Bud Tucker; Jon Arnett, one of the greatest running backs in USC history who could have been a Heisman winner; Fred Gallagher, who always brought copious notes to the booth; and Jim Perry and Don Anderson, two of USC's esteemed sports information directors who came with me.

For the USFL broadcast, it was Rich Marotta, who may have been as well prepared as any color man I've been with and was a great partner on many boxing telecasts, and Kermit Alexander, the former UCLA great who made me an equal-opportunity partner.

With the San Diego Chargers, it was John DeMott.

In baseball, there's John Jackson, an All-American in both football and baseball, one of today's talented young broadcasters, and the son of one of the great USC assistant football coaches, and Jeff Proctor, a

ACKNOWLEDGMENTS

bright Georgetown grad involved in the Internet who has now hired me. Thank God for that.

In basketball, Jerry West, Kurt Rambis, and Michael Cooper, three former Lakers greats, must be included, along with Jerry Tarkanian, Rick Barry, who did the 1967 ABA All-Star game in Indianapolis with me, and Pete Newell, a true legend.

For high school football with Vootage, it's Garry Paskwietz, a great USC guy who knows every player around, and for basketball, it's Kris Johnson, the son of Marcus Johnson, who'd remind me of his playing on UCLA's national title team in '95.

In swimming, Janet Evans, who held every record for years and went to Stanford, worked with me on some events. In track and field, Carol Lewis, Dwight Stones, and Tom Feuer, one of the big gears now at Fox Sports Net, helped me out.

Others in the booth I must add are: Gene Whitlock, who I'd introduce as "your downtown, international insurance broker"; Jay Berman, Doug Mann, and the late Dennis Minishian, who'd hand me a stat just as I was thinking about it; Dr. Bob Francis, who always had a camera and was more accurate than I was in deciding who had made a tackle; Jim Raser, a producer way back in the beginning; and Sandy Vonhof, Riley Ridderbush, and Orin Sampson.

A thank you to our dearly departed Giles and Ollie Pellerin, who saw more USC games than anyone else in history. Ollie loved to play golf, and we'd play all over the country.

I continue to do many golf shows, and the main man is Andy Thuney, the head pro at Hacienda Golf Club in LaHabra Heights, who keeps me on the straight and narrow.

Also, many thanks to: Pat McClenahan, my partner in *Video Gold*; Dave Levy; and Nick Pappas and his wife, Deedee, great friends of USC and loyal Trojans since the days of Howard Jones.

My four children are also important in my life. As most fathers do, I regret the moments when we couldn't spend as much time together. My moving around was no excuse, but I owe them a debt of thanks for putting up with me. My oldest daughter, Kathy, has been in many ways my best friend, always looking out for me. My other daughter, Colleen, and my sons, Chris and Kevin, have also given me five grandchildren and many warm moments. I hope I've been the kind of father and grandfather they've wanted me to be.

I also owe gratitude to my wife, Danuska. Although she still thinks of football as soccer and doesn't quite understand some of the things I've done, she sure enjoys reminiscing about all these moments.

A special thanks to the powers that be at USC—in particular, Tim Tessalone, who is without a doubt the best at what he does. I was recently honored by the L.A. County Board of Supervisors as one of the most recognizable voices in the history of Southern California sports. I felt proud to be included in that same group with Dick Enberg, Vin Scully, Chick Hearn, and Bob Miller. During the middle of a busy day, Tim attended that session. I appreciate his friendship and help through the years. It's easy to be a broadcaster when those ad-libs are simple to come by. That's what Tim does. To him and others at the university, you have my deep vote of thanks.

Writing a book that covers five decades at Southern California has been a thought of mine for a long time, and Tom Hoffarth asked if he thought we should do this project together. So I'm grateful to him for his invaluable help and the writing skills he's exhibited here.

Most of all, I'm indebted to the fans of the University of Southern California and beyond. To the people whose games I saw that gave me thrill after thrill after thrill, it's like a fairy tale. I could not have asked for a better scenario. I still love going to today's games, watching the fans, being recognized by them, and being asked for an autograph or picture.

I've had a wonderful time—Simply unforgettable and maybe more or better than I deserve. To all who had a hand in making it a great run, I'm indebted. Thank you, God bless, and fight on.

—TOM KELLY

ACKNOWLEDGMENTS

This project was much more than just turning on a tape recorder and letting Tom Kelly spin stories for hours upon hours. From the very start, the goal was to make sure the reader could hear Tom's voice on every page. My only regret is that we couldn't include a CD of his famous calls or expand the *Trojan Video Gold* series into a DVD, updating it from the 1988 season. Those are definitely on my to-do list in the near future.

For this book, a special thanks goes first to Jeff Proctor, who was the connection in setting up a story about Tom's career for the *Los Angeles Daily News*. The idea to write a book blossomed from that story, and we're all thankful it did.

Tim Tessalone, USC's longtime sports information director, and Steve Lopes, USC's associate athletic director, supported this from the start and opened the holes. Tim was somehow able to take time out from his legendary beach volleyball career to double check important statistical information and provide contacts for many of the people who contributed personal stories about Tom. Mike Garrett's recollection, a finishing touch, was very appreciated, and Craig Fertig's foreword was worth waiting for.

Pat McClenahan, Tom's co-producer on *Video Gold*, provided more insight and assistance, and countless individuals contributed to the "celebrity roast," which turned out to be Chapter 12.

Thanks to Joe Jares, esteemed USC journalism professor and former *Daily News* colleague, and to Jay Berman, Kelly's former stat man, former *Daily Breeze* newspaper colleague, and a decent softball pitcher in his day, for doing a great deal of raw editing on both names and dates.

To Bob Miller, the Kings' Hall of Fame play-by-play man and another legendary voice of Southern California sports, and to Steve Springer for their professional guidance on how to publish a book in three months or less.

To my amazing wife, Rhonda, and my well-grounded kids, Andrew and Hannah, for helping me stay sane, which isn't easy. Same goes to the *Daily News* powers that be: Ron Kaye, Melissa Lalum, Gene Warnick, Matt McHale, and Kevin Modesti.

And, of course, to the Voice of the Trojans, for allowing me to find out what a true gentleman and kind-hearted man he really is. Listening to Tom animatedly relive some of Southern California's most exciting moments at the Riviera Country Club players' lounge was like hearing history come alive. Tom Kelly will always be the soundtrack to everything that is USC, and now I have the audiotapes to enjoy for years to come.

—TOM HOFFARTH

INDEX

A
Aaron, Hank 4
Abrams, Adam 109
Achica, George 26, 86
Adams, Pete 106
Affholter, Erik 88, 108
Against All Odds 147
Aikman, Troy 88, 89
Akron Goodyear Wingfoots 6
Albert, Frankie 65
Alcindor, Lew 48
Alcott, Amy 142
Alexander, Kermit 190
Allen, George 133
Allen, Marcus 25, 26, 76, 86, 87, 99, 173
Allice, Ron 53
Altenberg, Kurt 88
Amateur Athletic Union 6, 39
Ameche, Alan 148
Anderson, Don 190
Anderson, Flipper 88
Andros, Dee 95
Andrusyshyn, Zenon 74
Antonio, Marco 180
Antonovich, Mike 189
Anything Goes 138
Appel, Chris 44
Arbogast, Pete 160
Arizona State University 40, 108
Arnett, Jon 190
Ashby, Verne 44
Auburn University 55
Auerbach, Red 149
Avery, Chip 157
Ayala, Ron 97, 109

B
Baltusrol Golf Club 23
Bame, Damon 101, 159
Banks, Chip 26, 87
Barker, Bob 138
Barnes, Billy 70, 154
Barry, Brent 123
Barry, Rick 121, 191
Barry, Sam 39
Bartlesville Phillips 66 Oilers 6
Bartner, Dr. Arthur 42
Barty, Billy 93
Bashore, Rick 98
Baylor University 109
Beard, Frank 142
Beathard 12, 65, 154
Beathard, Pete 11, 12,17, 64, 65, 92, 93, 102, 105, 154,159
Beban, Gary 74, 75,88, 188
Bedsole, Hal 17, 64, 102, 105, 159
Bell, Bobby 70
Bell, David 109
Bell, Ricky 25, 81, 83, 86, 87, 107
Benirschke, Rolf 116, 125
Berman, Jay 191, 193
Bibby, Henry 51, 52
Blanda, George 152
Boise State University 36
Boston Celtics 149
Boy Meets World 148
Boyd, Bob 45, 46, 47, 48, 49
Bradley University 4, 6, 7, 141
Bradley, Foster 53
Brickhouse, Jack 4
Bridges, Jeff 147
Brocklin, Norm Van 131
Brooks, Albert 148
Brown, Dale 47
Brown, Jim 162
Brown, Willie 65, 86, 159, 177
Browner, Joey 26
Bryant, Bear 32, 76, 77, 78
Buck, Jack 7, 8
Budde, Brad 26, 86
Buford, Don 43
Bullard, Ed 53
Buoniconti, Nick 68
Bush, George H.W. 40
Bush, Jim 53
Bush, Reggie 70, 88, 101
Butcher, Dennis 149
Butcher, Ron 64
Butz, Jerry 145

C
Caley, Charles 6, 9
Caray, Harry 7
Carey, Tony 102
Carrier, Mark 34, 89, 107
Carroll, Pete viii, 26, 35, 36, 37
Carter, Allen 82, 107
Casanova, Len 72
Case, Everett 45, 46
Cashman, Pat 74, 104
Chandler, Bobby 106
Channel 11 126
Chapman College 48
Chargers 56, 115, 119, 124, 126, 188
Chicago Bears 136, 152
Chicago White Sox 149
Clark, Don 30, 72
Clausen, Casey 155
Cleveland Browns 86
Clinton, Bill 139, 140
Cobb, Marvin 80
Colter, Cleveland 107
Cooper, Michael 191
Corleone, Michael 146
Corp, Aaron 155
Coryell 123, 124
Coryell, Don 33, 123
Couples, Fred 173
Cowboy in Africa 148
Cowlings, Al 76
Crane, Bob 186
Crawley, Rex 52
Crookendon, Ian 53
Crosby, Bing 142, 144
Crowder, Eddie 93
Crutcher, Fred 108
Cunningham, Sam "Bam" 76, 77, 79, 83, 106, 155
Cusano, Mark 27

D
Daily News 193, 194
Daland, Peter 53

TOM KELLY'S TALES FROM THE USC TROJANS

Dallas Cowboys 45
Damone, Vic 144
Daniels, Bill 126
Darby, Matt 90
Daugherty, Duffy 20
David, Larry 144
Davidson, Ben 152
Davis, Anthony 79, 80, 81, 82, 83, 86, 87, 106, 107, 157, 165
Davis, Clarence 76, 86, 106
Davis Jr, Sammy 144
Dayton Air Gems 6
Dean, Dizzy 44
Dedeaux, Rod 17, 38, 39, 40, 41, 42, 43, 48
DeKraai, Terry 97
Del Rio, Jack 26
DeMott, John 126, 190
Dewey, Thomas 140
Dickerson, Sam 88, 105
Diggs, Shelton 80, 82, 107
Doggett, Jerry 129
Donahue, Terry 47, 87, 171
Dorsett, Tony 85
Drake University 4, 6
Drake, Ducky 187
Drees, Jack 6, 7, 15
Drury, Morley 70
Drysdale, Don 153
Duke University 22
Dummit, Dennis 104
Dunphy, Jerry 136

E
Edwards, Dennis 86
Einhorn, Eddie 149
Elliott, Ray 9
Elway, John 169
Emanuel, Aaron 108, 155
Enberg, Dick 138, 176, 185, 192
Enyart, Bill "Earthquake" 95
Ervins, Ricky 100, 108
Evans, Janet 191
Evans, Vince 25, 107
Evashevski, Forest 134

F
Falk, Peter 144
Fargas, Justin 118
Farmer, George 74
Fears, Tom 131
Ferguson, Vagas 70
Fertig, Craig v, vi, 32, 59, 67, 68, 69, 93, 94, 102, 103, 106, 117, 118, 151, 152, 166, 177, 190, 193
Feuer, Tom 191
Fields, Kenny 186
Fisher, Jeff 99
Fisk, Bill 20, 102
Flaherty, Mike 3
Florida State University 23, 151, 152
Floyd, Tim 49, 52
Flutie, Doug 126
Fonda, Henry 142
Foster, DeShawn 118
Foster, Roy 26, 86
Fouts, Dan 104, 116, 124
Francis, Dr. Bill 62
Francis, Dr. Bob 165, 166, 172, 191
Frank Sinatra Open 142
Frankenheimer, John 147
Fraser, Brendan 148
Frazier, Walt 151
Fresno State University 27, 36, 121
Furillo, Bud 25, 187, 190

G
Gallagher, Fred 190
Gallery, Tom 65
Garagiola, Joe 7
Garrett, Mike 65, 67, 69, 70, 71, 75, 88, 92, 93, 94, 103, 118, 159, 173, 190, 193
Gathers, Hank 49
Geiberger, Al 53
George, Ray 61
Georgia Tech University 12, 13
Gibbs, Joe 123
Gifford, Frank 150, 151
Gillespie, Mike 53
Gillman, Sid 128

Glazer, Paul Michael 144
Goeddeke, George 95
Golf the West 146, 173
Goodrich, Gail 46
Goodwin, Tom 168
Goux, Marv 22, 25, 28, 29, 30, 31, 33, 165, 177
Gowdy, Curt 69, 178
Grady, Steve 94
Graf, Allan 106
Grant, Bud 1
Green, Gaston 88
Greene, Cornelius 79
Greene, Danny 145
Griffin, Archie 79, 81, 82
Grossman, Ken 130
Gunn, Jimmy 104

H
Hackett, Paul 37
Hackford, Taylor 147
Haden, Pat 80, 82, 83, 84, 107, 157
Hadl, John 127
Halas, George 136
Hale, Chris 155
Hall, Charlie 71
Hall, Monty 137, 138, 139
Hanlon, Tom 136
Hanum, Alex 44
Hardy, Kevin 103, 104
Harmon, Tom 134, 136, 137
Haskins, Don 120
Hatos, Steve 138
Hawkeyes 91
Hayes, Woody 79, 81, 82, 93, 94
Hazzard, Walt 46
Healy, Jim 186
Hearn, Chick iv, vii, 6, 7, 11, , 12, 13, 15, 158, 160, 185, 192
Helinski, Florian 148
Heller, Ron 64, 91
Herald Examiner, 190
Here's Lucy 148
Hiestand, Bob 129
Highlights of USC's 1964 Football Season 158

INDEX

Hill, Fred 64, 67, 68, 102
Hill, Jesse vii, 9, 11, 12
Hillman, Pete 44
Hipp, Eric 99, 109
Hirsch, Elroy "Crazylegs" 131, 132, 133
Hirsh, Jack 46
Hoffa, James R. 145
Hogan, Ben 137
Hogan, Todd 2
Hope, Bob 142, 143, 144

Howard, Ken 144
Huarte, John 62, 63, 67, 68, 69
Hubbard, President 25
Hull, Mike 104

I
Indiana University 47, 74, 100, 148
Iverson, Allen 122

J
Jackson, John 190
Jackson, Keith 81
Jares, Joe 193
Jeter, Gary 36
John Wooden's Pyramid of Success 188
John, Jill St. 144
Johnson, Keyshawn 108
Johnson, Kris 191
Johnson, Marcus 191
Johnson, Norm 86
Johnson, Randy 43
Johnson, Tom 102
Jones, Howard 9, 73, 191
Jones, Jimmy 76, 88, 98, 105, 106
Jordan, Frank 98, 109, 176, 177
Joyce, Father 59, 60
Joyner, Charlie 125

K
KABC 186
Kansas City Chiefs 70, 118
Kansas State University 113
Kaye, Ron 194
KCAL 180
Kelcher, Louie 125

Kelley, Bob 9, 131
Kelley, Rich 120
Kelly, Danuska 40, 189, 192
Kelly, Jim 126
Kelly-Borisoff, Kathy 180
Kennedy, John F. 139
Kerlan, Dr. Bob 147
Kern, Rex 79
Keyes, LeRoy 75
Kimble, Bo 49
King, Bill 6
Kingman, Dave 43
Kirkpatrick, Dennis 171
Kirner, Gary 104
Klein, Bob 104
Klein, Mal 142
Klosterman, Don 126, 128
KMOX 7
KMPC 131
Knight, Bob 47
Knox, Elyse 134
KNX radio 7, 9, 49, 65, 115, 123, 126, 131, 132, 134, 137, 142, 147, 153, 158, 180, 186, 187
KNX-TV Channel 2 136
Koch, Howard 147
KOGO Channel 10 123, 126
Krause, Ed "Moose" 62
KSDO 126
KTTV Channel 11 130, 142, 152
Kuller, Fred 104

L
L.A. Express USFL 112, 113, 128, 126, 147
Lalum, Melissa 194
Lamonica, Darryl 58
Larrabee, Mike 52
Las Vegas SportsView 162
Lasorda, Tommy 43
Leach, Dick 53
Leahy, Frank 56, 58, 59
Leinart, Matt 101
Leon, Clayton de 157
Leslie, Lisa 54
Let's Make A Deal 137, 138
Levy, Dave 20, 22, 33, 81, 123, 166, 177, 191

Lewis, Carol 191
Lewis, Tommy 49
Licotta, Lenny 145
Limahelu, Chris 109
Lloyd, Vince 4
Long Beach State 121
Long, Dallas 52
Lopes, Steve 193
Los Angeles Daily News 193
Los Angeles Dodgers 9, 128, 129, 130, 131, 156, 157, 158, 160
Los Angeles Lakers 7, 11, 111, 119, 126, 158, 160 ,183
Los Angeles Rams 21, 26, 29, 33, 98, 131, 133, 134, 136
Los Angeles Times 9, 90, 158
Lott, Ronnie 26, 107, 169
Louis, Joe 180
Louisiana State University 47, 166
Luigi, J.J. Di 155
Lupo, Tom 17, 102
Lutz, Bob 53
Lynn, Fred 43
Lynn, Johnnie 98, 106

M
Madden, John 25
Maddox, Tommy 89
Magee, Jerry 187
Mann, Doug 191
Mantle, Mickey 42
Marbury, Stephon 122
Margerum, Ken 169
Marino, Dan 128
Marinovich, Todd 89, 90, 100, 108
Marotta, Rich 126, 179, 190
Marquette University 46, 151
Martin, Dean 142, 144
Martin, George 180
Martin, Gordie 44
Martin, Rod 107
Mason, Bobby Joe 149
Mathis, Johnny 144
Matthews, Bo 113
Matthews, Bruce 26
McAlister, James 98

TOM KELLY'S TALES FROM THE USC TROJANS

McClenahan, Pat 22, 191, 193
McClenehan-Kelly Productions 162
McCord, Gary 137
McCullouch, Earl "The Pearl" 74, 75, 104
McDonald, Paul 25, 166, 190
McGee twins 54
McGuirck, Pat vii, 7, 8, 9, 115, 65, 92, 113, 132
McGuire, Al 46
McGuire, Frank 151
McGwire, Mark 43
McHale, Matt 194
McKay, J.K. 82, 107
McKay, John iv, vi, vii, 11, 12, 14, 15,16, 17, 19, 20, 21, 22, 23, 24, 25, 26, 29, 30, 32, 33, 35, 36, 37, 44, 47, 56, 60, 61, 65, 68, 69, 72, 73, 74, 75, 76, 77, 78, 79, 80, 82, 83, 84, 90, 91, 93, 94, 95, 97, 98, 102, 104, 106, 107, 130, 159, 160, 177, 178, 185
McKenzie, Dave 145
McNeil, Freeman 99
McNeill, Rod 106
Meador, Eddie 133
Meadows, Audrey 92
Miami Dolphins 125
Michaels, Al 176
Michaels, Bob 141
Michigan State University 20, 35, 95, 100, 119
Miller, Bob 192, 193
Miller, Cheryl 54
Miller, Chuck 4
Miller, Lennox 104
Milwaukee Allen-Bradleys 6
Minishian, Dennis 191
Minnesota Vikings 1
Minor, Harold 49, 50
Mississippi State University 48
Missouri Valley Conference 7
Mitchell, John 78
Modesti, Kevin 194
Montana, Joe 109
Morgan, J.D. 106
Morrison, Marion 94

Morrison, Stan 49
Morton, Craig 69
Morton, Johnnie 89
Mosebar, Don 26
Moton, Dave 103
Mulligan, Billy 45, 46
Muncie, Chuck 22, 124
Munoz, Anthony 26, 85

N

National Basketball Association 6
National Industrial Basketball League 6
Navy 92
Nelsen, Bill 11, 12, 17, 56, 102, 105
Nelson, Lindsay 154, 178
Ness, Elliott 177
New York Knicks 51
Newbury, Dave 109
Newell, Pete 6, 47, 119, 120, 121, 191
Neyland, General Bob 154
Nixon, Richard 140
North Carolina State University 45, 46
Northwestern University 108
Notre Dame iv, 17, 21, 22, 27, 29, 50, 55, 56, 58, 59, 60, 61, 67, 68, 69, 72, 73, 80, 81, 82, 83, 95, 102, 103, 108, 109, 113, 147, 157, 158, 165, 166, 168, 169, 178, 179

O

O'Malley, Peter 130
O'Malley, Walter 128, 129
Oakland A's 6
Oakland Raiders 6, 25, 87, 106, 107, 152
Obradovich, Jim 83
Ohio State University 21, 55, 70, 78, 79, 81, 82, 83, 85, 93, 94, 167
ON-TV 111
Oregon State University vi, 22, 67, 95, 97, 118, 122
Otten, Brad 108

P

Pacino, Al 146
Page, Alan 68

Page, Toby 74, 75
Palmer, Carson 101
Papadakis, John 177
Pappas, Nick 14, 191
Parker, Artimus 107
Parker, Charlie 50
Parseghian, Ara 69, 81, 95
Paskwietz, Garry 191
Paterno, Joe 100
Patterson, Red 128, 130
Peckinpah, Sam 104
Peete, Rodney 34, 88, 89
Pellerin, Ollie 191
Penn State University 26, 87, 99, 100, 116
Peoria Caterpillars 4, 8
Pepperdine University 32
Perry, Dick 47, 48
Perry, Jim 168, 171, 190
Phillips, Charles 80
Phoenix Mercury 153
Pierce College 128
Pitt 85
Pitts, ZaSu 134
Pittsburgh Pirates 9
Pittsburgh Steelers 125
Polamalu, Troy 90
Posten, Tom 151
Preece, Steve 95
Princeton University 23
Proctor, Jeff 155, 163, 165, 190, 193
Prothro, Tommy 33, 47, 75, 98, 113, 123
Psaltis, Tony 45
Pullman University 100
Purdue University 22, 72, 95, 167
Putnam, George 19

Q

Quarrie, Don 52
Quinlan, Jack 4

R

Raaphorst, Dick Van 93
Rae, Mike 79, 83, 98, 106
Raines, Chris 156
Ralston, John 31, 109
Rambis, Kurt 191

INDEX

Ramirez, Raul 53
Ramsey, Tom 86
Randolph, Sam 53
Raser, Jim 191
Raveling, George 49, 50
Reade, Lynn 102
Reischling, Kyle 174
Rice, Bruce 136
Richter, Pat 64
Ridderbush, Riley 115, 191
Robinson, John 25, 26, 27, 28, 29, 30, 33, 35, 36, 47, 86, 99, 107, 108, 118, 160, 169, 171, 190
Rockne, Knute 55, 59, 60 , 62
Rodriguez, Quin 109, 158
Rogers, Danny 38
Rogers, Johnny 97
Rogers, Pepper 47, 98
Rosenthal, Dick 59, 60
Rossovich, Tim 31
Roth, Hyman 146
Rothstein, Arnold 146
Royster, Mazio 35, 108
Rudometkin, John 44
Rutter, Darrell 146

S

Sagouspe, Larry 93
Sajak, Pat 138
Sale of the Century 7
Salisbury, Sean 108
Sampson, Orin 191
San Diego Chargers 33, 104, 113, 116, 123, 152, 187, 190
San Diego Rockets 119
San Diego Union 187
San Francisco Warriors 6
Sanders, Barry 89
Sanders, Red 9, 22, 33, 154
Saroni, Al 29
Saukko, Richard 130
Scheider, Roy 147
Schembechler, Bo 26
Schenkel, Chris 178
Schrader, Loel 25
Schroeder, Jay 99

Scully, Vin 129, 138, 156, 158, 160, 176, 185, 192
Seagren, Bob 52
Seattle Seahawks 113
Seaver, Tom 43
Selleck, Tom 48
Shafer, Don 109
Sharman, Bill 44
Sharp, Linda 54
Shaw, Nate 104
Sherman, Rod 67, 68, 69, 102, 103
Shula, Don 125
Sikking, James 144
Simonian, Don 13, 14
Simpson, O.J. 29, 31, 52, 70, 72, 73, 74, 75, 76, 79, 94, 95, 97, 104, 140
Sinatra Frank 143, 144
Six, Bob 92
Skinner, Bob 9
Skladany, Tom 83
Slaughter, Fred 46
Smalley, Roy 43
Smith, Dennis 26
Smith, Kevin 89
Smith, Larry 27, 34, 35, 108
Smith, Rick 188
Smith, Stan 53
Southern Methodist University 13
Snell, Matt 93
Snow, Jack 63, 68
Sogge, Steve 74, 97
Southern California Sports Broadcasters Association 172
Southern California Sports Broadcasters Hall of Fame 153
Southern Illinois University 151
Spitz, Mark 53
Springer, Steve 193
St. Louis Cardinals 7, 8, 44
Stadler, Craig 53
Stagg, Michael 158
Stanford University 22, 24, 109, 120, 132, 145, 169, 191
Stanley, Ken 44
Staubach, Roger 92
Stockton, Dave 53

Stones, Dwight 53, 191
Strasberg, Lee 146
Stratton, Gil 136
Stratton, Susan 180
Strother, Deon 108
Sutton, Bob 9
Svihus, Bob 102
Symes, Bill 65, 190

T

Taft, Skip 41
Tampa Bay Buccaneers 22
Tarkanian, Jerry 121, 123, 191
Taylor, Greg 174
Tennant, John 145
Tessalone, Tim 170, 192, 193
Texas A&M University 22
The Bob Crane Show 129
The Fall Guy 148
The Fourth War 147
The Godfather, Part II 146, 157
The Price is Right 138
The Scout 148
The Way It Was 69
The White Shadow 144
This Week in Southern California Sports 174, 175
Thuney, Andy 146, 191
Tinsley, Scott 108
Toley, George 53
Tollner, Ted 33, 34
Topping, Dr. Norman 14, 67
Townsell, Jojo 126
Trojan Magazine 51
Trojan Video Gold 106, 162, 188, 193
Truman, Harry 139
Tucci brothers 142
Tucker, Bud 187, 190
Turner, Booker 187
Turner, Eric 88
Turning of the Tide 177
Twogood, Forrest 38, 43, 44, 45

U

UC Irvine 46
UCLA 6, 9, 14, 22, 27, 32, 33, 37, 45, 46,

48, 49, 50, 51, 53, 55, 71, 73, 74,
86, 87, 88, 89, 90, 91, 95, 98, 99,
105, 106, 107, 140, 148, 151, 153, 154,
171, 175, 176, 177, 186, 187, 188, 190,
191
University of Alabama 17, 32, 55, 76, 77, 167
University of Arizona 34, 167
University of Arkansas 167
University of California 22, 24, 49, 102, 119, 120,158
University of Colorado 92, 93, 109
University of Illinois 4
University of Iowa 22, 91, 100
University Miami 125
University of Michigan 26, 55, 67, 70, 85, 106, 118, 134
University of Minnesota 40, 55
University of Missouri 25
University of Nevada-Las Vegas 121
University of Nebraska 97
University of North Carolina 36, 52
University of Oklahoma 55
University of Oregon 22, 72
University of San Francisco 119
University of Southern California vii, 118
University of Tennessee 99, 154
University of Texas 48, 55, 94, 97
University of Texas-El Paso 120
University of Utah 36
University of Washington 86, 104
University of Wisconsin 55, 64, 65, 67, 69, 131, 186
Uplinger, Hal 150
USC Athletic Hall of Fame v, 16, 24, 38, 44, 53, 118, 172
USC Sports Magazine 173
Ussery, Charles 86
Utah State University 30, 31

V
Valvano, Jim 46
Van Horne, Keith 26, 85
VanderKelen, Ron 64, 65
Variety Club Children's Charity 138
Vataha, Randy 100

Verna, Tony 150
Vonhof, Sandy 191
Vootage.com 149, 155, 163, 165, 191

W
Wagoner, Darrell E. 158
Walden, Mike 65, 165
Walker, Herschel 126
Walton, Mark 173
Ward, Rachel 147
Warfield, Paul 93
Warner, Curt 100
Warnick, Gene 194
Washington State University 22, 50, 86, 88, 100, 164
Washington, Delon 108
Waterfield, Bob 131
Watson, Dennis 145
Watson, Jim 175
WATW 1, 2
Wayne, John 94
Weaver, Charlie 104
WEBC 3, 140
Weismuller, Johnny 144
Wellman, Gary 100, 108
West, Jerry 191
Westphal, Paul 49
What's My Line? 151
Wheel of Fortune 138
Whitaker, Jack 137
White, Charles 25, 26, 85, 86, 87
White, LenDale 70
White, Reggie 126
Whitlock, Gene 191
Williams, Andy 137, 142
Williams, Randy 52
Wilson, Ben 67, 154
Winchell, Walter 177
Winfield, Dave 40
Winslow, Troy 104
Winter, Tex 44
Wise, Robert 145
WMBD 4, 149
WNBA 153
Wolfe, Vern 52, 53
Wood, Richard 36
Wood, Stan 53

Wooden, John 39, 45, 188

Y
Young, Adrian 72, 73
Young, Charlie 106, 107, 140
Young, Steve 126, 127, 128

Z
Zela, Lou 145
Zeno, Larry 107
Zimmerman, Gary 126